SINGLE-SESSION

@

ONLINEVENTS

CW01096017

SINGLE-SESSION THERAPY
@
ONLINEVENTS

Windy Dryden

Onlinevents Publications

Contents

Preface   vii

PART I   INTRODUCTION   **9**
1   Single-Session Therapy   11
2   Single-Session Therapy at Onlinevents   37

PART II   THE CONVERSATIONS   **43**
3   Helping the Person to Get Unstuck   45
4   Helping the Person to Address Guilt   62
5   Prompting Mum to Get a Connection   80
6   Helping the Person to Accept the Cacophony
    of Feelings Towards Her Mother   101
7   Helping the Person to Assert a Boundary
    with Her Father   120
8   Helping the Person to Address Procrastination   137
9   Helping a Person to Integrate Different Parts
    of Herself   157
10 Developing a Plan for the Person to Accept
    Herself in Birmingham   173
11 Helping the Person to Address Performance
    Anxiety   194
12 Helping the Person to Trust that Her Mother
    Will Say One Thing and Do Another   214
References   233
Index   235

Preface

The Covid-19 pandemic has had a profound influence on many aspects of life. In the world of counselling and psychotherapy it has shown us that we can continue our work virtually with our clients using Zoom and other online platforms when previously we questioned whether we could do so. I have personally been surprised concerning how well my clients and I have adapted to this way of working. However, it is in the field of the training and education of counsellors and therapists that online events have come into their own, particularly in offering continuous professional development events to many who would have struggled to attend these events pre-Covid.

Let's take as an example the two-hour online continuous professional development (CPD) events that I do for Onlinevents on single-session therapy (SST) which are the subject of this book. Once a month, I do an hour's lecture on a relevant mental health topic and show how this problem area can be addressed using the insights from SST. I then do two SST demonstrations with volunteer members of the online audience who are currently struggling with a personal issue relevant to the topic of the evening.

Onlinevents suggests a fee for the evening but people are encouraged to pay what they can afford which results in a large virtual audience for an event which has at times exceeded 500 people. Would this have occurred if Covid-19 had not forced us to adjust to the very difficult times it has brought in its wake? I doubt it. Virtual CPD will become the norm. Why travel for CPD when you can get it in the comfort of your own home?

It is against this backdrop that this book came about. As I describe in Chapter 2, the CPD training I currently give on SST for Onlinevents lasts for two hours. In the first hour, I give a PowerPoint presentation where I first briefly outline SST and show how it can be applied to a particular topic area. Then I do two SST sessions with volunteers on problems related to the evening's theme.

In the first part of the book, I give an outline of SST both in general and how I practise it in the Onlinevents context. Then, in the second part of the book, I present transcripts of ten sessions that I did between May 2020 and March 2021, together with my ongoing commentary of the work that I did in each session. I invited all ten people to add their reflections for inclusion at the end of each conversation and nine accepted the invitation with the other person declining on the grounds of ill-health.

I am very grateful to the volunteers for granting permission for their session with me to be included in this book and for providing their reflections. I also want to thank John Wilson and all at Onlinevents not only for making this book possible, but for providing me with the opportunity to bring my work to an international online audience.

I hope this book shows the potential of SST to help people make important changes in a very short period of time and John Wilson and I both hope that you can join us at our SST events in the future.

Windy Dryden
June 2021
London & Eastbourne

PART I

INTRODUCTION

1

Single-Session Therapy

Introduction

In the late 1990s, I read a book entitled *Single Session Therapy: Maximising the Effect of the First (and Often Only) Therapeutic Encounter* by Moshe Talmon (1990), an Israeli psychologist. While I found the book interesting, I did not resonate with it and, in any case, my professional focus was elsewhere at that time. As I approached retirement from my university post, roughly fifteen years later, I was looking for a fresh challenge. Of all the professional activities I engaged in, I most enjoyed doing live demonstrations of therapy when I gave a professional workshop. I have always thought that it was important for workshop leaders to demonstrate their points and, in my case, I endeavoured to do live demonstrations on whichever topic I was addressing in my workshop.

It occurred to me that in doing such demonstrations, I was practising single-session therapy (SST) and given this realisation, I re-read Talmon's book with fresh eyes. This time I did resonate with the ideas that Talmon was conveying. So, for the past eight years or so, I have devoted much of my professional time practising SST, training others in it and, of course, I continue to do live demonstrations of how I practise SST whenever I train, as long as it is practical to do so.

Before, I discuss my SST work for Onlinevents CPD in Chapter 2, which is the focus of this book, let me outline some salient features of single-session therapy or SST as I will refer to it throughout this book.

Definition of Single-Session Therapy

I define SST as 'an intentional enterprise where the client and therapist set out on the understanding that (a) the therapist will endeavour to help the client to achieve what they have come for in one visit and (b) more help is available to the client if needed'.

This definition has several features that are worth emphasising:

SST Has a Therapeutic Purpose

It is not practised in order to reduce an agency's waiting lists or waiting time for potential clients, although these may be the effects of introducing SST into an agency's service provision.

SST Is a Fully Contracted Form of Therapy

This means that both the client and the therapist give their consent to proceed based on a full understanding of what SST can do and cannot do.

SST Seeks to Integrate Two Seemingly Different Positions

While some people argue that SST should only involve a single session of therapy, the definition that I have put forward indicates that while the intention of the therapist to help the client in one visit, further help is available if needed. Thus, in SST we integrate two seemingly disparate points: (i) help the client in one session; (ii) provide the client with more help if needed.

The Nature of SST

SST is not an approach to therapy in the way that cognitive behaviour therapy or person centred therapy are therapeutic approaches. Indeed, therapists from a wide range of therapeutic approaches can and do practise SST (Hoyt and Talmon, 2014). Rather, SST is a way of thinking about therapy sometimes referred to as single-session thinking (Hoyt, Young and Rycroft, 2020, 2021) or the single-session mindset (Young, 2018). SST can also be seen as a way of delivering services in the same way ongoing therapy and blocks of therapy sessions are. I will discuss the single-session mindset and SST service delivery later in this chapter.

SST is based on the idea that a brief encounter between two persons can be therapeutic and that the length of therapy is expandable.

The Three Major Foundations of SST

SST is based on three major research and practice findings.

1. The most frequent number of sessions (known as the 'mode') clients have internationally is '1', followed by '2', '3', etc. This occurs across a range of public and charitable therapy agencies.[1] When people hear

[1] It is not known whether this also occurs in private practice although one of my American colleagues who runs a part-time

this they immediately assume that this means that the clients ended therapy because they did not find it helpful.

2. However, 70–80 per cent of those who have one session are satisfied with that session given their current circumstances.

3. Therapists are poor at predicting who will attend for only one session and who will attend for more, a finding that has significant clinical and organisational implications. This also means that it is not possible to judge in advance who will benefit from SST and who will require more help

Favourable Conditions for SST

I sometimes refer to SST as a plant. A plant needs certain conditions to flourish and if it does not get these conditions it will wither. The following are, in my view, the main conditions needed for SST to grow and develop.

Help Is Provided Quickly in Response to Help Being Sought

The effectiveness of SST depends, in large part, on the client being ready to address their problem with the therapist. The longer the client has to wait for help to begin, the more their motivation to change dissipates and the less likely they are going to engage with the therapist to address their nominated concern. This is why it is an oxymoron for a client to be placed on a lengthy waiting list for SST.

---

practice and keeps meticulous client data was shocked to discover that the mode in his practice was also '1'.

Time Between Help-Seeking and the Appointment is Used Well

As I will discuss presently, SST can be by walk-in or by appointment (Hoyt, Bobele, Slive, Young and Talmon, 2018). In walk-in SST, the client is seen as soon as a therapist is available to see them. Normally, the client will have to wait for approximately 30–60 minutes to be seen. In appointment-based SST, ideally the wait for an appointment should ideally be as short as possible. The aim should be for the client to be seen 2–3 days after an appointment has been made. In both cases, the time between help-seeking and the appointment should be used profitably mainly to help the client to prepare for the session. This is done by the client completing a pre-session questionnaire designed to help them focus on what they want to discuss with the therapist and what they want to achieve from the discussion. If possible, this questionnaire should be shared with the therapist so that they can also prepare for the session.

Both Therapist and Client Hold Realistic Expectations about SST

Many counsellors think that very little can be achieved in a single session. However, in my view, it is possible for the therapist to help the client find a meaningful solution to their nominated concern and to develop a plan to implement this. On the other hand, it is very unlikely that the therapist is likely to help the client effect a quantum change i.e., a sudden, dramatic, and enduring transformation that affects a broad range of emotion, cognition, and behaviour.

The Importance of Informed Consent

As I noted above, SST is a fully contracted form of therapy and a lot of its potency comes from what the client brings to the process. Consequently, it is vital that the client comes with a full understanding of the nature and purpose of SST and fully engages with the work of the session.

Therapy Begins Immediately

Perhaps the most therapeutically potent feature of SST is that therapy begins immediately. Thus, the immediate emphasis is on the therapist and client working together to help the client address a concern selected by them and walk away from the session with something meaningful that equips them to deal effectively with this concern. Anything that interferes with this immediate therapy focus such as client assessment, history-taking and case formulation is avoided. Having said this, it is true that many therapy agencies require therapists to undertake various activities with all clients such as risk assessment and data collection for research and evaluation purposes. If this is the case, then the therapist is mandated to carry out these activities as part of their job. However, once these tasks have been one, they can then help the person focus on their nominated concern and work towards their session goal.

Organisational and Administrative Support Is Provided

When SST is incorporated into the range of services offered by a delivery of a therapy agency, then for it to survive and thrive in that agency, several agency-related conditions need to be present to help it do so.

First, it is important that people in the agency have a working understanding of SST and have an opportunity to discuss any doubts, reservations and objections (DROs) that they may have to SST. These DROs need to be respectfully listened to by advocates of SST and responded to with sensitivity. SST needs to be disseminated to potential clients clearly and with enthusiasm and this is only possible if agency workers are positively disposed towards SST.

Second, it is important that SST is only practised by therapists who want to practise it. Nobody, clients and therapists alike, should have SST imposed upon them. If therapists are compelled to practise SST when they don't want to they will become antagonistic and this will affect negatively the working atmosphere within the agency.

Third, therapists should be properly trained in SST and have their ongoing SST practice supervised by more experienced SST practitioners. If this does not happen then therapists' skills will become stagnant and affect their work negatively. Thus, an agency should preferably be willing to fund proper training and ongoing supervision for SST to flourish in an agency.

Finally, SST should be well supported administratively. It is important that administrative staff are educated to understand SST and trained to convey it accurately to clients seeking help from an agency and want to find out what services the agency offers.

'Help Provided at the Point of Need' Is Based on Several Ideas

I mentioned earlier that SST is based on providing help at the point of client need. This way of delivering therapy services is based on the following ideas:

- It is better to respond to client need by providing some help straight away rather than by waiting to provide the best possible help. In sum, 'sooner is better'. However, if accurate information about waiting times is made clear, a client can be invited to have a single session immediately or wait for the best possible help.
- Providing immediate help is more important than carrying out an assessment or a case formulation.
- Therapy can be initiated in the absence of a case history.
- People have the resources to make use of help provided at the point of need.
- The best way to see if a client will respond well to SST is by offering them SST and see how they respond.
- Therapy can be initiated immediately and risk managed if this becomes an issue.
- Appropriate therapy length is best determined by the client.
- When a person does not return for another session this may well indicate that the person is satisfied with what they achieved, although it may be the case that they were dissatisfied with the help provided.

The Therapist's Goals in SST

As mentioned earlier, the main goal of SST is for the therapist to help the client achieve their stated wants by the end of the session.

It is also possible to consider outcome and process SST goals from the therapist's perspective as follows:

The Therapist's Outcome Goals

- To help the client get 'unstuck'.
- To help the client take a few steps forward which may help them to travel the rest of the journey without professional assistance.

The Therapist's Process Goals

These goals point to what the therapist aims to do in the session to enable the client's outcome goals to be met. They reflect the fact that there is more than one way of the client's outcome goals to be achieved.

- To help the client address a specific concern.
- To give the client the space and opportunity to think and explore when needed.
- To help the client see that they have the wherewithal to achieve their goals.
- To help the client select a possible solution.
- To give the client the experience of the solution in the session, if possible.
- To help the client develop an action plan.

Ways of Delivering SST

There are several ways in which SST can be delivered by an agency which I will now discuss.

Referral to SST Based on Suitability Assessment

Here, SST is delivered to people who have been assessed as being suitable for it. This way of delivering SST is based on what might be termed 'conventional clinical thinking'. Here inclusion criteria are drawn up which clients need to meet in order to receive SST. In addition, exclusion criteria are drawn up which 'exclude' people from being referred to SST. While clients might be given a say concerning their wish to access SST, the bulk of the responsibility for 'placing' clients to the 'most suitable' form of help for their presenting concern rests on the shoulders of the agency-employed assessor.

This approach to SST service delivery is the one that is at most odds with 'single-session thinking' for several reasons. First, the time spent on making a suitability assessment can be better spent offering a person a therapy session based on their stated wants. Second, the walk-in SST literature shows us that it is not clear at all who may benefit from SST and who may not before the person has a single session. As such the best way of discovering who will benefit from SST is to give people a single session of therapy and see who will benefit, remembering that more help is available for those who do not benefit. Third, this approach is based on the idea that the professional knows better about what the person needs than the person themself. As will be discussed presently, SST is based on the view that the person themself can be trusted to choose whether or not they think they can benefit from this service delivery mode.

Walk-in SST

As the name makes clear, walk-in therapy '[e]nables clients to meet with a mental health professional at their moment of choosing. There is no red tape, no triage, no intake process, no wait list, and no wait. There is no formal assessment, no formal diagnostic process, just one hour of therapy focused on clients' stated wants .... Also, with walk-in therapy there are no missed appointments or cancellations, thereby increasing efficiency' (Slive, McElheran and Lawson, 2008: 6).

In this mode of service delivery, by arriving at a walk-in therapy clinic, the client has determined that they can potentially benefit for a single session of therapy, a view not challenged by the therapist whom they are seeing.

Integrate SST into the Agency's Service Provision and Promote Client Choice

A third way in which an agency can deliver SST is bring SST to sit alongside other modes of service delivery and have the client choose which service they wish to access, a decision that is honoured by the agency unless there is a good clinical reason not to do so. For this approach to work, the agency needs to do two things. First, it needs to provide full and accurate information about each of the services that it offers to enable the client to make an informed choice. Second, it needs to give the client current information about the time that they may need to wait to access each of the services being offered.

The 'Gateway' or 'Embedded' Approach

The final way in which an agency can deliver SST is to embed SST fully into its service delivery which is itself based fully on single-session thinking. How this works is as follows. The agency makes clear that instead of the traditional first point of entry for a client where they would have an initial meeting with an agency worker to assess their treatment needs, this initial point of contact is based on a treatment session focused on that client's stated wants. This is known either as the 'embedded' approach (because SST is fully embedded into the agency's approach to helping clients) or the 'gateway' approach (because all clients are offered a treatment session as their gateway into the agency). If this approach is taken by an agency, the following points need to be made clear to incoming clients.

1. People in general want therapeutic help at their first point of contact with an agency rather than that first visit being taken up with an assessment for therapeutic help which is initiated at a later date.
2. When clients are offered a therapy session at their first visit it has been shown that for 50 per cent that session is sufficient and for 50 per cent further help is requested.
3. The most reliable and valid way of discovering which group a client falls into is after a single session has been completed rather than before.
4. If a client needs more help after the single session, the nature of that help will often become clearer on completion of a treatment session than at the end of an assessment session.
5. The client will be able to access further help usually after a period of reflection at a follow-up session or earlier if needed.

Single-Session Thinking and Good Practice

The most effective way of practising SST, in my view, is to base this practice on single-session thinking (sometimes known as the single-session mindset) rather than on conventional clinical thinking. In this section, I will show how single-session thinking informs good practice in SST.

Create a Realistic Expectation for SST

An expectation refers to a conviction held by a person that something will happen. Single-session thinking suggest that the SST practitioner should strive to create a realistic expectation that the client can take away something meaningful from the session that they can implement to improve their life in certain ways. Additionally, the end of the session is not the end of the process but the beginning of one that the client can take forward. What the practitioner should refrain from doing is conveying to the client that (a) nothing meaningful can come from a single session; (b) the client will be 'cured' in some way or (c) the client will experience a quantum change (i.e. a sudden, dramatic, and enduring transformation that profoundly affects a broad range of personal emotion, cognition, and behaviour).

Utilise the Power of 'Now'

Single-session thinking emphasises that when a therapist meets with a client then all the therapist knows is that they are with that person 'now'. They do not whether they will see the client again even if the two have contracted for longer-term work. Given this, the therapist and client need to decide how to best use what may be the only time that they will meet. Do they want to spend that time carrying out an assessment of the client's problems pending treatment of those problems some time in the future, for example? Or do they want to spend the time focusing on the client's nominated concern looking for some way to resolve this issue? Single-session thinking promotes the latter rather than the former, assuming that the client concurs.

Be Client-Centred

Single-session thinking stresses that the client should be at the heart of therapeutic work. This means that the therapist should ask the client what issue that want to discuss and what they want to get from the conversation. Then the therapist should ensure that the two work together to help the client to achieve what they have come for.

Engage the Client Quickly Through the Work

People often express the doubt that an effective working alliance can be formed in SST. Their point is that a therapeutic relationship needs time to develop. Both research and SST practice show that this doubt is not substantiated. For example, in a research study, Simon, Imel, Ludman, and Steinfeld (2012) showed that clients who benefitted from a single session of therapy had developed a good working alliance with their therapists and those who did not benefit from SST did develop such an alliance. From a practice perspective, by eliciting what a client wants to discuss in a single session, by focusing on this issue and by eliciting and working towards what the client wants to take away from the session, the SST practitioner is able quickly to form an effective alliance with the client. This alliance is also strengthened by the therapist demonstrating their keenness to help the client as quickly as possible.

Develop an End of Session Goal

If you recall, SST is based on the therapist integrating two ideas: helping the client in one session given that the therapist does not know whether they are going to see the client again and providing the client with more help if needed. What gives the session shape is helping the client to work towards what they want to take away from that session. Given this, the SST practitioner generally asks the client at the outset such questions as:

- 'What would you like to take away from the session that would make your attendance today worthwhile?'
- 'If you reflect on the session this evening and you conclude that you were really glad you came today, what would you have achieved that would have led you to this conclusion?'
- 'If you got what you came for today and decided that you don't need to come back, what would you be taking away?'

'ONE THING'

It is important that the therapist does not overload the client in SST. Thus, helping the client to take away one thing from the session that is meaningful for them is better than helping them to take away several things that may lead to confusion and be easily forgotten. Single-session thinking encourages the principle of 'one thing' and the effective SST practitioner is guided by this principle throughout the session (Keller and Papasan, 2012).

SESSION GOAL VS PROBLEM-RELATED GOAL
I find it useful to distinguish between a session goal and a problem-related goal. The former relates to what the client realistically hopes to achieve from the session, while the latter relates to what the client sees as a good outcome with respect to their problem. As I will discuss presently, the client's session goal often turns out to be the solution which if implemented helps the client to achieve their problem-related goal.

Determine the Best Helping Stance with the Client

In SST there is no one helping stance that characterises this mode of service delivery. Rather, there are a range of possible helping stances that a therapist can adopt to help the person with what they have come for. These include:

- Focusing on the client's nominated concern and helping them to find a solution to this concern.

- Helping the client to explore an issue to facilitate better understanding.

- Encouraging the client to express suppressed feelings.

- Helping the client to explore their options and helping them to make a decision that they need to make.

Given that SST is client centred (see above), it is important that the client selects the therapeutic stance that they think will best help them with what they have come for. Thus, discussion of helping stances is best done after the client has nominates a session goal. If necessary, the therapist should outline these helping stances for the client so that the latter can make an informed choice.

Agree a Focus for the Session with the Client

A client may bring several to the session and if so, the therapist needs to help them to focus on one. This may involve the therapist encouraging the client to select one of the issues that they have brought or it may involve the two of them selecting a theme that is common to all the presented issues. Whichever is the case, it is important that the therapist and client agree a focus for the session. This focus may be narrow (e.g. dealing with a specific concern and searching for a specific solution) or it might be broad (e.g. exploring the client's feelings about an issue to gain greater understanding).

Keep on Track

Once a focus has been agreed, it is the therapist's responsibility to help the client maintain this focus. This may involve the therapist tactfully interrupting the client (a practice which is best done once the client has given prior permission for the therapist to do so). It may also involve the therapist checking periodically with the client that the two of them are discussing what the client wishes to discuss. Sometimes a focus may change, and it is important for the therapy dyad to decide whether to return to the previous focus or change to the new one. Frequent changes of focus are one sign that the client may need further help going forward.

Keep Up a Good Therapeutic Pace and Stop When Finished

Therapists new to SST tend to think that they have to rush 'to get everything in.' First, there is no set amount to get into a session. Single sessions vary according to how much ground is covered. Second, it is best to go at the client's pace. If a client processes information quickly then the therapist's pace would be quicker than if a client is slower in this respect. The main issue here for the therapist to consider is to go at a pace that facilitates helping the client to achieve their session goal.

This point also explains why it is better to finish a session when such a goal has been reached rather at the end of an arbitrary time period. This is why in my regular single-session practice I say that a session may last up to 50 minutes. Thus, if the client and I have done our work in 40 minutes we will stop at this point. If we continue for another ten minutes, then the impact of the session may be diluted.

As I will discuss in Chapter 2, in my single-session work for Onlinevents, I aim to complete a session in 25 minutes since I have an hour to conduct two such sessions with volunteers and allow for a short Q&A period. In fact, the ten sessions that appear in Chapters 3–12 lasted between 13 mins 59 secs and 22 mins 54 secs.

Be Clear and Foster Clarity

In my experience, effective SST practitioners not only work at a pace that facilitates client learning (see above), they also are clear in their communications and encourage the client to be similarly clear, particularly if they, the therapist, does not understand anything that the client has said. Therapist clarity occurs at various junctures throughout the session.

- At the very beginning the therapist makes clear what they can do and can't do in SST and that more help is available to the client if needed.
- The therapist helps the client to be clear about what they want to achieve from the session and how they think that the therapist can best help them to do this.
- If the client is looking for a solution to a problem, the therapist clarifies what solution-based options are available to them and helps them to be clear about what they need to do after the session to implement a selected solution.
- By contrast, if the client is looking to understand an issue better without necessarily seeking a solution, the therapist helps them to gain greater clarity on this issue.
- Towards the end of the session, the therapist encourages the client to summarise the work that they have done together so that the client can be clear about what they are going to be taking away from the session.
- Finally, at the end of the session, the therapist reiterates clearly that the client can have further

help in the future, if needed, and how they can access such help.

Make an Emotional Impact

Ideally, the therapist should work towards making an emotional impact on the client at salient points in the session. If the discussion is purely theoretical and the client's emotions are not engaged, then the two will have an interesting conversation, but nothing will change. Conversely, if the client is overwhelmed with affect, then they will not be able to think clearly about what is being discussed. When this happens, it is a marker that the client will need more help after the single session has been completed, which, of course, should be offered to them. The ideal state to aim for is when the client is able to think clearly about the therapeutic focus with their emotions appropriately engaged. Another way of putting this is that the client's head and heart are working in tandem. Having said this, the therapist should not artificially push to make such an emotional impact on the client since this usually backfires. Rather, the therapist should look for and respond to occasions when the client's affect has been naturally engaged while discussing personally meaningful material.

Identify and Utilise the Client's Strengths

SST can be seen as part of a therapeutic movement where the therapist is encouraged to focus on and use the client's strengths in therapy rather than focus on and repair their deficits. Single-session thinking argues that the client has many internal strengths, but that they may have lost contact with these. Consequently, the therapist seeks to reintroduce the client with that part of themself that is resourceful and in doing so encourage them to reflect on how they might use these strengths to deal with the concern for which they are seeking help from SST. I usually explain to clients that a person's strengths may be 'tough-minded' (e.g. grit, resilience or perseverance) or 'tender-minded' (e.g. compassion, kindness and empathy). The person can offer these latter tender-minded strengths to themself as well as to others.[2]

Encourage the Client to Use Environmental Resources

Single-session thinking agrees with the phrase, 'only you can do it, but you don't have to do it alone'. As such, the single-session therapist will encourage the client to think of their environment as offering helpful resources to aid them as they address their nominated issue. Such resources include other people (e.g. who might provide the client with emotional or other forms of support), agencies (who may offer relevant forms of guidance related to the client's problem) and self-help material in the form of 'apps' and printed material.

Identify and Utilise the Client's Previous Attempts to Deal with the Problem

It is very likely that the client has previously tried to solve the problem for which they are seeking help from SST.

---

[2] Most of the volunteers for SST@Onlinevents CPD are counsellors. When asked about their strengths, they often mention that they have such tender-minded strengths which they offer to others, but they are not so good at offering these qualities to themselves, a fact that often becomes the basis of a solution to their nominated problems.

While it is probable that on balance these attempts ere unsuccessful, there may have been elements that were helpful, at least potentially. Therefore, it is useful if the therapist asks the client to relate their past attempts to solve the problem, utilising the helpful elements and distancing themself from the unhelpful elements. In doing so, it may be productive for the therapist to help the client to understand why their previous attempts to solve the problem were unsuccessful and doing the opposite may contribute to the solution of the problem.

Negotiate a Solution

When the client is seeking help for an emotional problem and after the SST practitioner has helped them to set a goal for the session, the two of them embark on a search for a solution. To my mind, an effective solution addresses the client's problem and encourages them to achieve their problem-related goal. It often happens that the client's solution is a more specific version of the session goal. I illustrate this on the next page.

The therapist and client use a variety of sources in developing a solution. These include: (i) helpful elements of the client's past attempts to solving the problem; (ii) the therapist's and client's joint understanding of what accounts for the problem, the opposite serving to provide a solution to this problem; (iii) the client's strengths; and (iv) external resources that the client may utilise.

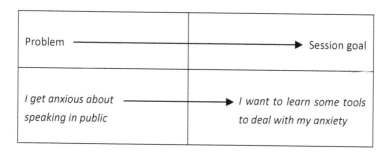

Problem ——————————————————►	Session goal
I get anxious about speaking in public ——————►	I want to learn some tools to deal with my anxiety

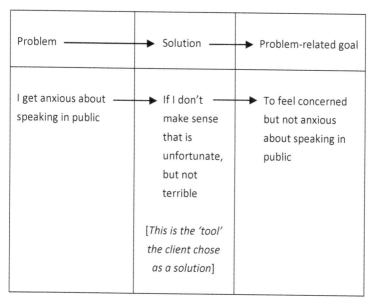

Problem ————►	Solution ————►	Problem-related goal
I get anxious about speaking in public ————►	If I don't make sense that is unfortunate, but not terrible [This is the 'tool' the client chose as a solution]	To feel concerned but not anxious about speaking in public

Encourage the Client to Rehearse the Solution

In the same way that a person takes a car out for a test drive before buying it, the single-session therapist encourages the client to rehearse the solution to see how it 'feels'. This may lead to a 'tweaking' of the solution or the selection of a different solution. Imagery, chairwork and role-play are examples of how the client may be invited to rehearse their chosen solution.

Help the Client to Develop an Action Plan

Once the client has settled on a solution and rehearsed it, the therapist then helps the person to develop an action plan so that they can implement the solution in their everyday life. An action plan involves the client specifying when they are going to implement the plan, in which circumstances and how frequently. The most important point about the plan is that the client can integrate it into their everyday life so that they can implement it regularly.

The therapist should ideally help the client to anticipate and address effectively any obstacles to the implementation of their devised action plan. Using imagery to gain experience of dealing successfully with such obstacles is particularly helpful here.

Encourage the Client to Summarise

Therapists have generally been taught that it is helpful to summarise periodically the work that they have done with their clients in sessions. This idea reflects 'conventional clinical thinking'. By contrast, given that single-session thinking suggests that the therapist encourages the client to be active throughout the session, the former asks the latter to summarise the work that they have done in the session. This indicates that the session is coming to an end. When the client summarises the work done in the session, they indicate what stands out for them and what they are going to take away from the session. The summary should ideally reflect the solution and any principle that is related to the solution. The therapist may want to add to the client's summary if the client has, in the therapist's view, omitted a salient point. Inviting the client to make a written note of this principle and/or solution can be particularly useful as a record and reminder of what the client will take away from the session.

End Well

Jerome Frank (1961) argued that while clients come to therapy seeking help for a wide range of symptoms, a sense of 'feeling demoralised' often underpins these symptoms and are the driving force for help-seeking. Consequently, one of the goals of therapy is to restore a client's morale. This is certainly the case in SST where the emphasis is to help the client get unstuck and move forward with their life. Ending a single session well is a good way of helping a client to leave feeling remoralised. To do this the therapist needs to do the following things.

TIE UP LOOSE ENDS
One of the ways of ending a single session well is to tie-up any loose ends with the client. Inviting the client to mention something that they want to say or to ask the therapist is a good way of doing this. Care needs to be taken that the client does not bring up a new topic at the end and this is why I suggest that the therapist's invitation is limited to the focus of the session.

CLARIFY NEXT STEPS
There are a number of possible next steps that the client make take after a single session, including:

- Leaving the session happy that they have achieved what they have come for and being invited to contact the agency if they need further help.

- Engaging in what I call the 'reflect-digest-act-wait-decide' process. Here, the client is encouraged to reflect on what they have learned from the session, digest the learning, take action and let time pass before deciding whether or not to make another appointment.
- Being called by the agency after a short, specified time (e.g. three weeks) to determine how the client is getting on and to see whether or they need further help.
- Making an appointment for further help at the end of the session. This will be limited to help provided by the agency or that provided by another agency connected with the hosting agency. If possible, the client should be given accurate waiting times to access the relevant help.

Arrange Follow-up

In this context, a follow-up differs from an agency calling a client after a short, specified time to see how they are getting on with a view to offering them more help. It occurs after a longer period of time to get feedback on the effectiveness of SST and to get the client's views on the service they received and how it could be improved. While it also provides the client with an opportunity to ask for further help, this is not the main purpose of longer-term follow-up which is to evaluate outcome and improve service provision.

In the next chapter, I will discuss my practice of SST within the context of Onlinevents.

2
Single-Session Therapy at Onlinevents

In this chapter, I will discuss the work I have done on single-session therapy for an online counselling training organisation called 'Onlinevents'. This provides the context for the transcripts of single sessions that I conducted for Onlinevents which I will present and comment on in Chapters 3–12.

What Is Onlinevents?

Onlinevents is an online platform offering CPD to counsellors and psychotherapists. It operates a 'pay what you can' approach so that money should not be an obstacle to access to high quality CPD. Onlinevents' mission is 'is to provide affordable CPD for practitioners who are looking to top up their CPD hours and learn about a variety of topics'. In this respect Onlinevents has been particularly successful in lockdown due to Covid-19. It has provided a much-needed and well respected learning and collegial community where counsellors can enjoy the connection with authors, workshop facilitators and other colleagues.

SST at Onlinevents

The continuous professional development (CPD) training I have given on SST for Onlinevents have been two-hour events. In the first hour, I usually do a PowerPoint presentation where I first briefly outline SST and show how it can be applied to a topic area such as procrastination, dealing with difficulties with adult children, dealing with difficulties with parents, shame, guilt and anxiety. After answering questions at the end of the first hour, I conduct two single-session conversations in the second hour. These are with volunteers from the online audience who are prepared to discuss their concerns centring on the topic discussed in the first hour in front of the watching audience. My aim is to have a conversation with a volunteer that lasts for about 25 minutes, which leaves 5 minutes for a brief Q&A section with members of the audience.

It is important for me to stress here that the nature of SST at Onlinevents is different in two major respects from the nature of SST that is offered in clinical practice generally. First, an Onlinevents single session is shorter than a regular SST session. As shown in Chapter 1, the length of the ten conversations that appear in Chapters 3-12 of this book ranged from 13 mins 59 secs to 22 mins 54 secs with an average length of 19 mins 17 secs. Second, I will only be seeing the volunteer once for a single-session therapeutic conversation. This is known colloquially as a 'one-off' single session. This contrasts with regular SST where the therapist and client work together to help the person take away from the session what they came for, but knowing that more help is available if needed.

A Process View of SST Conversations at Onlinevents and My Therapeutic Goals

In Chapter 1, I presented an introduction to the routine practice of SST in the context of private practice or in an appointment-based agency (as opposed to a walk-in clinic). In this section, I will provide a process view of the single-session conversations that I have with Onlinevents volunteers together with my goals at each step.

It is important to note at the outset that while I keep the following points in mind, I emphasise some more than others in particular conversations and, indeed, some points may be omitted entirely. The following framework is just that – a framework. It is not a protocol that has to be followed in every conversation. In my experience, every conversation that I have with volunteers is different as you will see in Chapters 3–12.

CLARIFY PURPOSE OF CONVERSATION WITH CLIENT

In my brief outline of SST at the beginning of the first hour of my presentation, I make clear what the purpose of an SST conversation is. However, I usually like to begin each conversation that I have with a volunteer in the second hour of the presentation with a question concerning the person's understanding of the purpose of the conversation that we are going to have with one another. It is important that the person's understanding of the purpose of the conversation matches what I can offer and if not, it is important that I make transparent at the outset what I can do and what I cannot. If you recall from Chapter 1 such transparency is a key part of single-session thinking. In short, my goal here is to ensure that the volunteer has an accurate understanding of the purpose of the conversation that we are going to have together.

AGREE FOCUS, SET GOAL FOR CONVERSATION, RETAIN FOCUS

Given the short period of time I will have with the volunteer, it is vital that we both use this limited time well. My goal here is threefold.

First, I want to help the person to choose to discuss what is important to them and to focus on this throughout the session. Usually, this will be a particular concern that the person has. However, if they mention more than one concern that they want help with, I will ask them to select one such concern or to find a theme that is common to the concerns that they have mentioned. If they can identify such a theme, I will work with this in the session and doing so will become the focus. When taking this latter, theme-based approach, it is still important for me to help the person to discuss a specific example of their problematic theme. Otherwise, the conversation becomes too theoretical.

Second, after a focus has been established, I want to help the volunteer remain focused. This may involve me gently interrupting them to bring them back to the agreed focus.

Third, as it is important that the conversation has a therapeutic direction and as we only have a limited time together, I ask the person what they would like to achieve by the end of the conversation. This becomes the goal of the conversation.

WORK TO UNDERSTAND UNDERLYING PROCESS BEHIND CONCERN

I find that much of the conversation that I will have with the person is devoted to us working to understand the key mechanism that accounts for the existence of the person's concern and also how they may unwittingly maintain this concern. If we can develop a mutual understanding of such matters, then this paves the way forward for us to find a solution to the concern. During this part of the conversation, I will encourage the person to share their views on what accounts for the concern and its maintenance and I will also offer my understanding of these matters if the person is interested to hear them.

IDENTIFY SOLUTION AND INVITE PERSON TO REHEARSE IT IN SESSION

As noted in Chapter 1, several factors contribute to the development of a solution to the person's nominated concern. These include: (i) the understanding of the factors that explain the existence and maintenance of the concern and factors that may lead to a better outcome; (ii) helpful factors of the person's previous attempts to deal with the problem; and (iii) the internal and external resources available to the person.

Once a solution has been formulated, I invite the person to rehearse it in some way so that they can get a sense of the likelihood efficacy of the solution and whether they can imagine themself implementing it.

DEVELOP ACTION PLAN AND PROBLEM-SOLVE OBSTACLES

If time permits and it is relevant, I will discuss the importance of an action plan with the person the purpose of which is for them to implement to solution. If they foresee any obstacles to its implementation, these are identified and ways of addressing them are discussed.

END WELL

As with the clinical practice of SST, I endeavour to end the session well, asking the person to summarise the work we have done together and particularly what the person will take away from the session. I then ask the watching online audience for comments and questions.

The Conversations

In the next ten chapters I present transcripts of ten conversations that I have had with volunteers who have attended my SST online presentations at Onlinevents. Each volunteer sought help for a current issue. Please note the following:

1. Each volunteer has given their permission to have the transcript of our conversation published in this book.
2. I have changed the names of the volunteers.
3. I have provided periodic comments on each conversation to highlight various issues.
4. I sent each volunteer a copy of the transcript and invited them to provide written reflections on the conversation and what they got from it. Where the person accepted the invitation, these reflections appear at the end of the chapter.

PART II

THE CONVERSATIONS

3

Helping the Person to Get Unstuck

Windy – Steph: Interview on 11/05/20
Time: 17 minutes 6 secs

Windy: Hi Steph.

Steph: Hi Windy.

Windy: OK. How can I best help you today?

Steph: I am a bit stuck. I lost my brother two months ago and shortly after his husband confided in me and no one else that he'd found evidence of my brother having a seven-year affair and having sexual relations with other men, and it was a very difficult thing for me to hear and process. I feel I have processed it and found peace with it, but what I'm struggling with at the moment is it seems to be blocking me from communicating with my brother's husband. When I want to pick up the phone and speak to him and ask him how he's doing, I find it very hard to do that.

Windy: And, so, you say that you have processed that information.

Steph: Yeah.

Windy: Could you tell me a little bit about what that processing involved?

Steph: Yes.

Windy: What conclusion you came to?

Steph: I spoke to my personal counsellor, who I've recently ended with, but I was able to speak to her just before I ended, and... I was able to... [pause] get the information into perspective by seeing my brother as a whole rounded human being with flaws like the rest of us, and I felt I got... it in perspective... and... yeah. But what I'm left with is the devastation that his husband is left with and I'm the only one who he shared with and I feel a responsibility... towards him. I would like to offer him support, but it's hard.

Windy: OK. And, so, what would you like to get from this session that would have made it really worthwhile for you to have volunteered?

         [This is a typical question designed to help the person set a goal for the session.]

Steph: I think I would like to understand what's blocking me from communicating, because I want to talk with him and support him when he needs support.

Windy: OK. And, if you understand it, would you hope that you would then act on that understanding and be able to talk to him?

[When a person states that they seek 'understanding', I view this as a process goal and ask them for an outcome goal.]

Steph: Yes. I want to be able to speak to him, yeah.

Windy: OK. So, what conditions would have to exist, Steph, for you to do that?

[This is a typical intervention of mine. I seek to understand what conditions Steph thinks have to exist for her to be able to speak to her brother's husband.]

Steph: To speak to him?

Windy: Yeah.

Steph: ... *[Long pause]* I think... *[long pause]* I would need to be comfortable sharing my discomfort with him. So, I think what I'm saying is, it would have to be a two-way support rather than a one-way support. Does that make sense?

Windy: So, you would like him to support you as well as you to support him?

Steph: Yeah, a mutual support, because it's… [*pause*] information that's devastating for him, but it's also difficult for me. And, so, yeah.

Windy: Sure. You said, if I understood you correctly and I want to check with you, that you would want to be comfortable in sharing your discomfort with him.

Steph: Yes.

Windy: Is it possible for you to be uncomfortable in sharing your discomfort but still do it?

[*Having established that Steph has specified needing to be comfortable in sharing her discomfort with her brother's husband, I seek to discover how flexible she can be about this by asking her if it is possible for her to be uncomfortable about sharing her discomfort.*]

Steph: Yes, it is.

Windy: Yeah?

Steph: Yeah.

Windy: And, so, if you uncomfortably shared your discomfort with him and indicated to him that you did feel for him and you'd like to support him, but that you would like him to support you too, could you imagine doing that?

Steph: I can imagine doing that, but I can't imagine him supporting me. Maybe that's the issue.... We weren't close before my brother passed away. We didn't have a relationship, really. So, it's only a relationship that developed through my brother's illness and since his death.

Windy: And, so, if you said to him just that and you were uncomfortable saying that, but you would indicate to him that you would not only want to support him but you'd like him to support you, how would you handle him saying, 'Well, I'm not interested in that'?

Steph: That would be OK, actually, because I have many very good friends who I know I can confide in, who would support me. So, he's not the only one who can support me.

Windy: And how would you feel if he was pleased and would indicate that he wanted to support you?

Steph: That would be great, because that would... strengthen our relationship.

Windy: OK. So, let me put the pieces together.

Steph: Yeah.

Windy: So, at the moment, you're not speaking to him although you want to. You want to be comfortable about sharing your discomfort, but you recognise that you can do so uncomfortably.

Steph: Yes.

Windy: But, if you did and you indicated that you wanted support that was two-way and he said that he wasn't interested in that, that would be OK because you've got other people to support you and to speak to. If, however, he said that he would be interested in that, you would be pleased as well. So, I'm curious about, then, if we put all these things together. What's the missing piece of the puzzle that would lead you not to do that?

[I have been very careful to track what Steph has said and in doing so, it is not clear to me why she does not talk to her brother's husband.]

Steph: Not to pick up the phone and share my discomfort?

Windy: Yeah.

Steph: ... *[Long pause]* I don't know.... *[Pause]*

Windy: So, if I gave you one little ingredient that would lead you to do that, that you don't have, what would it be?

> [*This is another typical intervention of mine,
> 'What ingredient would you need to do what you
> say you want to do?'*]

Steph: ... [*Long pause*]

Windy: That could be an ingredient in you or in the world.

Steph: I think I know what it is. I think it's sharing with a friend what's happening... before I make the call; before I pick up the phone and speak to him.

> [*The 'ingredient' question helped take the conversation forward.*]

Windy: OK. So, if you shared with a friend first, then that would help you to do that?

Steph: Yeah. Yeah. I think the difficulty's been... sharing with a friend, in a way, feels... disloyal to my brother. So, yeah.

Windy: OK. So, at the moment, it sounds like there's a choice between you sharing with a friend first and for you to feel that that would be disloyal to your brother, or to not share it and to talk to his husband without sharing with a friend.

Steph: Hmm-mmm [*yes*].... [*Pause*] I think what I'm realising is I need some support around this. If I'm to offer support to him, I need support.

Windy: You need support.

Steph: I need support myself, not only from him, potentially, but from another source.

Windy: Just tell me a little about what your relationship was like with your brother.

Steph: With my brother?

Windy: Yeah.

Steph: ... [*Pause*] Very close growing up and close... [*pause*]. We moved apart into adolescence... but came together again as young adults, and he confided in me and it was a good relationship. And then, since I married and he married, sadly we grew apart and distant and very rarely spoke. But his illness was a long illness – he was ill for three months – and that gave me the opportunity to reconnect with him. So, before he died, we had become close again and shared an awful lot, and I'd expressed my regret that we had grown distant. So, yeah.

[I wanted to establish that Steph had a good relationship with her brother before asking her what he would want her to do.]

Windy: What would he want you to do?

Steph: He would want me to… [*pause*] do what was right for me.

Windy: Would he think that you talking about it to get support first was showing him disloyalty?

Steph: No, he wouldn't think that. No.

Windy: But you would?

Steph: … [*Pause*] Yes. I guess I fear others' judgment and I don't want my brother to be judged by others.

Windy: Right. So, you fear that, if you said to a friend about what you said, that they would judge him?

Steph: Judge him, yeah.

Windy: Is he older than you or younger than you?

Steph: Older, three years older.

Windy: Did he used to stick up for you when you were younger?

Steph: No.

Windy: Did you ever used to stick up for him when you were younger?

Steph: Yeah, because he suffered a lot of bullying.

          [*I have it in mind that Steph can be an advocate
          for her brother in the face of a judgment that
          another might make of him. It appears that she
          used to do that for him when they were
          younger.*]

Windy: Right. So, it's almost like that you want to
          protect his memory from bullying, in a way,
          from judgment.

Steph: Yeah, because he suffered an awful lot during
          his lifetime.

Windy: But I wonder what would happen if you shared
          it with a friend and he or she started to be
          negative about your brother. What would
          happen if you stood up for your brother with
          your friend?

Steph: That would be OK, yeah, and I'd feel... very
          comfortable doing that. I'm very able to do that.

Windy: So, it sounds like, Steph, that the reason you're
          stuck is that, if I was to put this in a chapter in
          terms of a book and chapters, and we've been
          unravelling this – Chapter 1 is that you are
          thinking about speaking to him and you've been
          uncomfortable; you're waiting until your
          comfortable to share your discomfort. And, as
          we've looked at it, you could ask for support

and, if he said no, then that wouldn't be so bad, and, if he said yes, that would be fab. But you need to actually speak about it with a friend too. Now, at that point you seem to have stopped going forward with the chapters, because, when I had the chapter which says, even if they do judge your brother, you could stand up for your brother.

[*I sometimes use the 'chapters in a book' metaphor to denote that what the volunteer is saying can be viewed as a process and that they get stuck because they close the book after a particular chapter. Encouraging Steph to keep the book open may help her to get unstuck.*]

Steph: … Yeah.

Windy: What about if you built that into the scenario, the narrative if you like?

Steph: Yeah. Yeah.... Yeah, that would feel good. Yeah.

Windy: Yeah?

Steph: Yeah.

Windy: So, why don't you summarise where we've got to at the moment, Steph?

[*Asking a volunteer to summarise the work we
have done so far helps to crystallise salient issue
for he person, as we will see.*]

Steph: … [*Long pause*] I want to communicate with my
brother-in-law because he has no one else to
share this with, but I'm feeling a difficulty. So,
I've realised that I need to be open with him and
say that I'm feeling some discomfort when I'm
talking to him and get his reaction.... If he says,
'I can't support you with this,' that's fine; I can
go and confide in a friend. If he says, 'Yes, let's
support each other in this,' that would be
wonderful; that would develop our relationship.
And… I've realised that, even though my
brother has passed away, I can still fight for him.

Windy: How do you feel when you really focus on that
idea: that, even though he's passed away, that
you could fight for him? How do you feel about
that?

Steph: Sorry, what do I feel?

Windy: Yeah, when you focused on that thought, on that
sense that you could still fight for him if the
person you chose to confide in to get support in,
in order to speak to your brother-in-law?

Steph: I feel quite empowered, actually.

Windy: Yeah?

Steph: Yeah. Yeah.

Windy: And, if you kept that sense of empowerment with you, what do you think you would do?

Steph: What do I think he would do?

Windy: What do you think you would do?

Steph: I would do.... *[Pause]* Now?

Windy: Yeah.

Steph: ... *[Pause]* I'd pick up the phone tomorrow and call my brother-in-law.

Windy: Having spoken to your friend first for support or not?

Steph: I think I can do it without doing that.

Windy: Right.

Steph: Yeah. And then, if I felt I needed support after speaking to him, then my friend would be there. So, yeah, I could do that.

[As can be seen, Steph found the idea that she could stand up for her brother empowering and seems to have lead to a shift in her.]

Windy: OK. So, let me take you through a guided imagery in terms of what you've been saying and let's see how you feel about this, OK? That you want to speak to your brother-in-law and you recognise that you're going to be uncomfortable doing so, but you recognise that you don't have to be comfortable in being uncomfortable; you can do it with discomfort, and that, with that sense of empowerment that you have, that whoever criticises your brother, you can defend him, that you would actually then take that sense and ring your brother-in-law.

[In single-session work, having the client rehearse the 'solution', whenever possible, is a useful way of having the client see if the 'solution' fits.]

Steph: … [Pause] Yeah.

Windy: Is that an accurate way of rehearsal?

Steph: Yeah.

Windy: You can imagine that, yeah?

Steph: Yeah.

Windy: OK.

Steph: It is, yeah.

Windy: Now, is there anything else that we need to talk about that we haven't yet, so that you think that you can actually get unstuck with this issue?

Steph: No. I feel I can move forward now.

Windy: Yeah? OK. Well, thank you for sharing with us, Steph.

Steph: Thank you, Windy.

Windy: OK, then. All the best. Take care.

Steph: Very powerful. Thank you.

[*As can be seen, Steph now feels that she 'can move forward' and that she found the experience 'very powerful'.*]

Steph's Reflections (29-05-21)

When I enrolled on Windy's workshop, SST seemed to me the antithesis of my own approach as a trainee counsellor, which relied on the building of a trusting therapeutic relationship over multiple sessions. I was intrigued – how could a client achieve progress in a single session? The powerful experience of joining with Windy in a demonstration session turned my scepticism on its head.

I felt the principles of equality and respect for autonomy were strong – the solution I reached was my own. Windy invited me to check it felt realistic and achievable and although he directed the pace and focused me by asking questions, I never felt he was leading or giving advice.

My difficulty was a block to communicating with my brother-in-law, following my brother's death and the discovery of devastating secrets. I was still grieving and the session inevitably touched on painful feelings, but Windy was skilful at keeping it moving, not dwelling on the deeper distress. This was the most significant difference I felt between SST and my experience of multiple humanistic counselling sessions: the focus on the goal as opposed to the movement towards pain. Some observers felt my distress had been ignored, invalidated; they were concerned for my wellbeing, checking on me via the chat room. But not addressing the deeper pain was ok for me. I knew before beginning the session that it was not about exploration of distress so I took note of the points that triggered emotion, knowing I could process them another time. For me, managing expectations is central to the ethical use of SST; being transparent about the solution-focused offer as opposed to the relational nature of other therapies.

There were two key moments for me during the session, the first being the realisation that I needed support with the heavy weight of secrets. This was precipitated by Windy's enquiries about what 'condition' or 'ingredient' needed to be present to unblock me. With hindsight, I had fallen into my default mode of rescuer, while ignoring my own needs. The second moment happened when Windy brought into the picture, the third person in the triangle – my brother – the 'victim' I was trying to protect and I identified that the fear of him being judged was blocking me from asking for the support I needed.

I did become unstuck following my single session. The proof of its efficacy is my communication with my brother-in-law later that week. I achieved my goal. But more than that, taking the first steps out of stuckness enabled me to move forward and fully process the cause of the block. Fear of judgment echoed the rejection my brother felt throughout his life. I felt deeply saddened by the secrets he carried alone and the missed opportunities to listen to my brother's story; to be there at his side to defend and support him. My acknowledgment of regret and shame was a significant part of my grieving process, directly facilitated by the single session. SST got me unstuck but also accelerated understanding of self – a liberating and empowering experience.

4

Helping the Person to Address Guilt

Windy – Grace: Interview on 29/06/20
Time: 16 minutes 8 secs

Windy: So, what's your understanding of why you're volunteering this evening?

Grace: Well, because I've got a bit of a dilemma and I would like some kind of solution, I suppose. Really, it's about trying to make myself feel better about a decision that I've actually made, or kind of a decision that I've made, really, about a very, very sensitive subject. So, it is really sensitive as well, just so that everybody else is aware. I don't want people screaming at me for this, alright?

Windy: OK.

Grace: Yeah. That's made everyone go, 'Ooh!'

Windy: I'll guarantee you that I'm not going to scream at you like this. I can't speak for the rest of them. OK.

Grace: OK, so, what it is, is I have a friend – I have had a friend for about three years now – whose husband is in prison. I don't know him, never met him, so I've only known her. She's got three kids. We get on great and everything else. Well, he's actually coming out of prison in October and he's a sex offender. So, that hasn't bothered me because she is believing that he is innocent and, if she believes him, that's fair enough. I believe her. I don't know about him, but I certainly believe her. Well, because it's now got out into the public domain that he's going to be released in October and they've put her address on Facebook and you can imagine people have been slagging her off and it's been absolutely awful. And I'm absolutely agonised over this because, obviously I'm a counsellor and, on the one hand, I've worked with sex offenders, I've worked with victims, so I kind of know both sides of it, and then, on the other hand, I'm supposed to be her friend and I don't feel very good about it because what do I do? I'm in a job in the local area where he's going to come to. I work at the local school and I'm really, really fearful that it's going to affect me. Just having the association with her or him, and I don't even know him, is going to affect me, and it's really, really frightened me. I've absolutely agonised over it.

Windy: So, did you say at the outset that you'd actually kind of made a decision?

Grace: I have. I had made a decision of sorts. I've been agonising over this for a couple of weeks, and she hadn't contacted me and I decided that I would give her a call and just say, 'Right, I know what's been going on.' I did make a call to her and said, 'Look, I know what's been going on. I've seen all the shit that's been going out on Facebook and social media and whatnot,' and I said, 'and I'm finding it really, really difficult.' I'm agonising about how I feel about it. I cannot imagine how she feels about it. She's been through this before and she's had to move. So, she's moved to near me from about 20 miles away. So, she's already been through this. It's been going on for her over and over and over. And, when she moved here, of course, it was all nice and quiet and nobody knew, and now they do. Because I didn't realise any of the ramifications of this, that it could be, until this all started up in the last two weeks, and it's really frightened me.

So, I did phone her and said, 'I know what's been said and I've seen it all,' and I said, 'I really agonised over it because I just don't know what to say to you and I don't know what to do.' And she said, 'I completely understand if you don't want to have contact with me.' And I felt really bad, and I said, 'I do want to have contact with you, but I don't know about any other contact other than on the phone, because I am afraid that it's going to affect my job at the school and in private practice and the fact that we live so near each other,' and all this. And I feel bad. I feel bad about it.

Windy: Which bit do you feel bad about?

[*I am aware that I did not ask Grace about what she wanted from the session. My sense is that this was due to the fairly long narrative that Grace made about her situation. I think I got caught up in this and forgot to ask for a session goal at the outset. I don't think that this omission unduly affected the work that we did with one another.*]

Grace: I think my fear of the ramifications; that it might affect me. And I know she's going through hell, and I suppose I feel bad about that and I'm thinking about me.

Windy: So, do you feel kind of badly because you're thinking about you?

Grace: Yeah, I think so.

Windy: In what way?

Grace: I think, as counsellors, we are expected to be the caring profession and we're expected to give our time and all of that, over the years. 'Well, you're a counsellor, you should know. You should be helping people,' and all of that. And, do you know what, sometimes I think, for me now, I've got to look after myself. I've got myself to think about too, do you know what I mean?

[*This theme comes up quite often in my single-session work with counsellors: 'On the one hand, I am a counsellor, and I am 'supposed to' help people and on the other, I am a person who needs to look after myself.' Often when a counsellor puts themself first, they experience guilt. Grace has not mentioned guilt yet, but this is the hypothesis that I have in my mind at this point of the conversation*]

Windy: So, having made that decision to look after yourself—

Grace: Yeah.

Windy: ...it sounds like there's some residual kind of bad feelings about that.

Grace: Yeah.

Windy: What would the feeling be? Could you identify the feeling?

Grace: Guilt? Guilt. Lots of guilt. Lots of loss, actually, loss of... a friendship. I don't feel like I'm a friend, you see. I think that's the biggest thing. What sort of a friend am I not to be supporting her? Do you know what I mean? I think that's why I feel guilty.

[*My hypothesis has been confirmed.*]

Windy: If I understand you correctly, and I just want to clarify that, what you seem to be saying is that you want to have contact with her over the phone...

Grace: Yeah.

Windy: ...it's just that – I don't know, did I understand that you feel that it might compromise you if you actually met with her and saw her in real life?

Grace: Yeah.

Windy: But your desire to want to have contact with her is still there.

Grace: Yeah, absolutely. I feel afraid to actually go and visit her or be with her just in our local area. If we were out of the area, that wouldn't be a problem. And the fact that I work at the local school, one of her children goes to that school also.

Windy: So, it sounds like that you feel badly because you've decided to look after yourself.

Grace: Yeah.... I just feel really guilty about it. I feel really bad about it.

Windy: What's your understanding of guilt in this sense? What kind of emotion is it for you?

Grace: Oh God.

Windy: What are the components?

[It is easy to assume that Grace and I share a common understanding on the nature of guilt. However, it is important for me to see whether or not this is the case. Hence, I asked Grace to spell out the components of guilt.]

Grace: The guilt of, really, not being able to support her at this time. She's on her own with three children, not that I was round there all the time, because I wasn't. I wasn't round there all the time. We didn't see each other all the time, but we certainly would see each other every month or something like that. But I just feel really bad that that is something that I feel that I can't do right now with this situation, and I feel like I don't want to meet him either.

[I note to myself that Grace has not answered my question. Rather she reiterates what she feels guilty about. I hold this mind as we go forward.]

Windy: No.

Grace: And I believe her when she says that he's innocent. She's absolutely stood by him because she absolutely believes he's innocent and they've put appeals in, and all this sort of stuff is going on, and I don't really understand it all. And I believe her.

Windy: So, if I understand you correctly, you do recognise that you do need to look after yourself, but the price of doing that is a recognition that you're not able to support her.

Grace: Yeah.

Windy: And you feel guilty about that. Is that correct?

Grace: Yeah.

Windy: Now, can I just clarify, because it's important that we both understand that we're talking about the same thing when we're talking about guilt? When you're feeling guilty, do you think you're a bad person for not being able to support her?

[Having asked Grace earlier an open-ended question about the components of guilt and not receiving an answer, this time I ask a theoretically-driven question, based on the conceptualisation which says guilt is 'I am not supporting my friend and I am a bad person for not doing so.']

Grace: Yes.

Windy: Yeah?

Grace: Yes.

Windy: What if we took that out of the equation? What if we put, in the equation instead, the idea that you're an ordinary human being who's really struggling to solve a very, very sensitive dilemma, but that you weren't a bad person? What difference would that make?

            [*Here, I am suggesting that Grace views herself as 'an ordinary human being' who is struggling in the face of a difficult dilemma rather than 'a bad person' who is not supporting her friend.*]

Grace: Well, do you know what, when you said that, it's like, if I took the counsellor hat off, take that out of the way altogether, that probably makes a really big difference, because I think, as a counsellor, I feel there's an expectation on us to be always caring and always supportive and always there and always have the answer, and all of that. If I take that off, yeah, I'm just an ordinary person like anybody else.

            [*My question seems to resonate with Grace and reveals the rigid view that she has about being a counsellor which she is bringing to the issue at hand.*]

Windy: And, if you were to get in touch with Grace the ordinary person, just focus on that, would that solve your dilemma?

Grace: … If I had Grace the ordinary person sitting in front of me, I'd be asking her why do I feel that that is my responsibility.

Windy: Alright. Well, ask her. Ask her.

Grace: Yeah. Why is it my responsibility? It's not my responsibility. It's not. It isn't my responsibility.

Windy: What are you responsible for in this situation?

[*Now that Grace has adopted the perspective of being an 'ordinary person', I invite her to think about what she is responsible for and what she is not responsible for in this situation. She would give a very different answer from the perspective of being 'I am a bad person.'*]

Grace: I guess I'm not responsible for what's happened. I can only support her from a distance, I suppose is what I'm saying. I can't be responsible for what's happened. I can't be responsible for how other people are reacting to her and to them and to him. I have to take myself out of the situation. I feel I have to take myself out of the situation, because I do not want to be in that. I don't want it.

Windy: But she knows that, in other circumstances, you would want…Well, you've told her that, even in these circumstances, you want to support her, but you can't do that at the moment because of the fear that it's going to be on your career. So, if you highlight Grace the ordinary person just for a moment, and then we come back to this idea that I want to see if I understand, because I must've missed something in my own counsellor education; I must've been absent for this lecture, the lecture that says that, once you're a counsellor, you have to be supportive to everybody no matter what. I must've missed that lecture. Where did you learn that?

[*I use quite a bit of humour in my single-session work. Here, I am questioning the idea that 'once you're a counsellor, you have to be supportive to everybody no matter what' by saying that I must have missed that lecture in my counsellor training.*]

Grace: I don't know.

Windy: Where did you learn that from, Grace?

Grace: I don't know. Do you know what, I think there's a bit of a culture, isn't there? When you look at all the BAC stuff and the counsellors together stuff and all the volunteer things and all this we're expected to do for nothing, you know what I mean? There's all this sort of culture that we live with. It always feels like there's an expectation that, because you're a counsellor, you are there to give help whenever anybody needs it, and I think that's what we all kind of learn and grow up with, not through our training, but through everything else around that.

Windy: Right, but we can question that.

[*Here, I do not go into the accuracy of Grace's views on what messages the counselling profession gives counsellors. Rather, I am encouraging to see that Grace can question such messages, true or not.*]

Grace: Yeah.

Windy: If that is the case, we could still question that and say, 'Actually, no. I don't have to live like that for myself.'

Grace: Yeah.

Windy: 'I am supportive, but there are times when I really have to prioritise myself.'

[*Here I am voicing a flexible position on this point. It would have been better if I had asked Grace to tell me what a flexible position on this issue would be for her.*]

Grace: Yeah.

Windy: So, it's like a flexibility thing in terms of you
               negotiating. This seems to be like saying, 'I'm
               Grace, I'm an ordinary human being, I'm going
               to look after myself.' 'No, I'm Grace, the
               counsellor. I have to support everybody.' And
               maybe, if you take that rigidity out of it and
               you're still left with the idea that it's important
               for you to care, but, certainly on this occasion,
               that you need to look after yourself.

Grace: Yeah, I do. And I think that is the right thing to
               do. I just want to feel OK about it.

Windy: OK about what?

Grace: OK about taking myself out of the situation. I
               don't want to be in the firing line.

Windy: Well, yeah, I understand that, but, in a way, the
               thing about guilt and the price to pay is that
               there is loss; that you aren't supporting your
               friend. And, so, I invite you to think that it's OK
               not to feel good about that.

               *[The term 'OK' seems so innocuous, but it often
               reveals that we are trying to make ourselves feel
               OK about an adversity. In my view, since an
               adversity is negative, it is constructive for us to
               experience a healthy negative emotion rather
               than an unhealthy negative emotion about it and*

rather than feel 'OK' about it'. This is an example of me bringing a therapeutic idea that I deem important to my single-session work with volunteers when it seems appropriate to do so.]

Grace: Yeah.

Windy: But to recognise that there's no ideal solution where you make a decision and you feel about all aspects of it.

Grace: I think I feel good about being honest with her, because even having that conversation was difficult, and I do feel good about that because I was honest.

[*In my experience when a person is 'under the influence of guilt', so to speak, it is difficult for them to access what they feel good about in the situation at hand. So, Grace's comment about what she feels good about is encouraging at this point.*]

Windy: Right.

Grace: So, I thought that's fair for her and I think she understood, but I also think that it's probably something she may well have heard before with other people.

Windy: Yeah.

Grace: And that may be the case. But I felt that it was important that I was honest with her and that felt better for me. And it was OK, and we had the conversation and it felt like it was OK.... I think it was the right thing to do. It was. I know it was.

Windy: Are you asking me or telling me?

Grace: No, I'm telling you. It was the right thing to do. I did the right thing. Yeah, absolutely.... But taking care of me instead of me taking care of her is a change because it is always I'm taking care of someone else. And, if I did have me sitting in front of me, I would be asking me, 'Why is it your responsibility?' and it's not. It's not my responsibility.

Windy: Right. Well, you could always have that conversation and, do you know something, Grace, you don't have to charge yourself. It's free.

[Here I note that while Grace may have not fully resolved the issue she can continue the conversation between the part of her that takes care of others and the part that needs to take care of herself that she has initiated in the above response.]

Grace: I'm too expensive, Windy. That's the problem.

Windy: Why don't you summarise the work that we've done so far tonight, Grace?

[*Again, I invite Grace to summarise the work we have done in the session. The time 'felt' right for me to ask her to do this at this point. I often go with my 'feeling' on when to ask volunteers to summarise our work.*]

Grace: Well, it's made me realise that, actually, it's OK not to be OK sometimes. It's OK to look after me and it's OK not to be responsible for everybody else. And it's the right thing to do to make sure that I'm OK and that I am taking care of me. So, that's good. That is good. I think it was the right thing to do.

Windy: Yeah, and I would just add that you are going to have some bad feelings about the loss and that you haven't decided to support your friend on this occasion, but that's the price, if you like.

[*Sometimes I decide to add a point to the volunteer's summary when I consider that they have omitted an important point.*]

Grace: Yeah.

Windy: There's no perfectly good outcome where everything is OK.

Grace: No. But maybe it will be one day, but not right now.

Windy: Maybe on the Planet Grace.

Grace: Maybe, yeah. OK.

Windy: Alright, OK.

Grace: Thank you.

Windy: Thank you.

Grace's Reflections (05-05-21)

I have thought about our session quite a bit, I think 'what am I, superwoman?'

This was a challenging situation where I felt guilt and responsibility to a friend. I didn't want to be judged by others negatively as was happening to her. The session highlighted these fears of being between a rock and a hard place whichever stance I took.

It made me realise that I wear the 'counsellor's hat' more than I should. I am only human and I don't have the answers, so why was I feeling so bad about this difficult situation? Well because I care about her, so it was emotional for me, being attached to someone causes feelings that sometimes are not good so 'break-ups' and 'loss' are painful. Talking to Windy helped me understand that it is not my duty to be the 'counsellor' all the time and that I have a responsibility to myself. This was a revelation when I realised this and saying these things out loud helped me hear it, also With Windy helping me to question myself allowed me to see I am the only one making the judgments on myself.

In the room with a client, I can bracket this off and I am very rarely affected emotionally which is what we are trained to manage. I have learned from listening to myself I was trying to find some kind of 'permission' to let her down, a friend would never do that. Actually, friends do that to each other, I hear this all the time in counselling.

Having the space to talk this through with Windy gave me freedom, I was scared initially to put it out there, but I felt supported and safe in a non-judgmental way. I was surprised that this could be achieved in one sitting!

I have accepted that I was not bad I was honest to us both. I was never her counsellor, that's not why we became friends in the first place, so she was not looking for a 'counsellor-like response' from me, what she got was me in my agonised and fragile feeling state, because of how I felt about her and the situation.

The session allowed me to think about me and not others for a change, what my needs were and how do I meet them. It's so nice to feel that I can have that too...which is what I try to offer people I work with, Thanks Windy for giving me that space, I will make sure that I give that to myself more often, the session helped me realise that too.

I have messaged her on occasion to see how she is, and her responses are brief, she may have chosen not to maintain some sort of contact with me and I'm ok with that.

I'm not bad, I'm human and I come first sometimes.

5

Prompting Mum
to Get a Connection

Windy – Carla: Interview on 27/07/20
Time: 22 minutes 54 secs

Windy: OK, Carla, thank you for volunteering this evening. Do you have a relationship issue that you would like some assistance with?

Carla: Yeah, it's my relationship with my mum I'd like to kind of bring.

Windy: And, should we be successful in helping you with that today, what would you have hoped to take away from our session to enable that to be successful for you going forward?

[Here I ask for the session goal as usual.]

Carla: I suppose what I'd like to take away is to develop a better way of feeling connected with my mum. I don't know if it's possible.

Windy: A better way of feeling connected to her.

80

Carla: Yeah.

Windy: And, so, at the moment, you're feeling disconnected?

Carla: Yeah. I think my mum's somebody that doesn't really show a lot of affect. That's probably the way, so you don't really know what she's thinking or feeling, and she was brought up in an orphanage, so it's already making me emotional.

Windy: Sure.

               [*Note that I acknowledge her emotionality without focusing on it. As it was so early in the session, I was not able to tie in her feelings with anything and wanted her to tell her story first.*]

Carla: My dad died last year and it's very difficult to… get how she's feeling or what's going on for her. She seems to be alright, but sometimes I'd like her to talk about those things with me, and that's where I feel the disconnect.

Windy: And have you told her what you'd like from her?

               [*I am thinking at this point that 'disconnect' results from two people, in this case, not talking to one another about anything meaningful. That is why I asked Carla if she had told her mother what she wanted from her.*]

Carla: I do from time to time but I think I do it with kind of humour. I kind of like to save any pain on my part.

[*So, Carla occasionally tells her mother what she wants from her but does so using humour to protect herself or her mother from pain. I'm not sure which yet.*]

Windy: OK. So, what do you think that might communicate to her?

Carla: It probably communicates to her that I'm alright and that it's not serious.

Windy: And, so, what do you think might happen if you communicated more of your true pain to her?

Carla: I'm a bit worried about upsetting her.

Windy: Because, if she became upset, what?

Carla: … [*Pause*] I just don't want to hurt her feelings. I don't want to have her worrying about me.

Windy: So, it's interesting that you want to connect with her, but you want to spare her feelings.

[So, this is Carla's dilemma. 'How can I connect with my mother while sparing her feelings?']

Carla: Yeah.

Windy: When you stand back and think about that, Carla, what do you think?

*[I **use** this quite often in my single-session work, inviting the client to stand back and reflect on what they have just said.]*

Carla: I think it's a bit daft, really; that I'm kind of avoiding upsetting her. I think, for me, I have a memory, when I was quite young, of my mum going to the doctor's and saying that she wanted to end her life. And I kind of think that I've always been frightened; I've always kept chipper with her and upbeat, because I can remember it really scaring me and I was about 12.

[This reflection leads to Carla having a very painful memory.]

Windy: Does she know how you feel about that?

Carla: I don't think I've ever told her about it.... No.

Windy: And what do you think would happen if you did?

Carla: I think she'd probably just dismiss it and be quite, 'Oh, that's silly dear.' I think that's kind of how she'd respond.... [*Pause*] I kind of feel she loves me, but sometimes I just want... [*pause*] more from her, sometimes, you know?

Windy: What would you like from her?

Carla: I'd like sometimes to have a little bit of an understanding of her inner world and when she's feeling good or she's not feeling good or, if she feels good all the time, that's fine. I'd just like her to talk about... herself a bit more, how she feels.

Windy: I'm sure she's not, but, if she was in the audience watching us this evening, what do you think her reaction would be to hearing you say that?

[When a volunteer is talking about another person, it is sometimes useful to get that person's view on salient matters through the eyes of the volunteer.]

Carla: I think she might be a bit shocked. Yeah, I think she might be a bit surprised. I think she might feel... probably a little bit hurt that I haven't said anything.

Windy: Can I ask you a question about what your view of connection in relationships is like? Do you have a model which says that connection should happen at the beginning or do you think you have a view which says connection can actually get deepened by you telling her things and her responding and you responding to her response and then her responding to your response?

[I remember thinking that I did not know what Carla's view of connection in relationships was and that knowing this might be helpful.]

Carla: I think I have an idea that connection is a little bit like a wave.

Windy: Yeah.

Carla: And that sometimes you feel it deeply and sometimes you don't feel it so much.

Windy: Yeah.

Carla: And sometimes it's about proximity, sometimes it's about sharing how you feel, sometimes it's just getting the other person. That's my idea of connection.

Windy: And, so, from what you've told me this evening about wanting, on the one hand, to find out about her inner world, but, on the other hand, wanting to protect her from pain, what do you make of your contribution to the wave of connection?

Carla: I think I probably hold back and just try and keep quite... [*pause*] upbeat a lot of the time.

[*This discussion leads Carla to state again that she holds back from her mother as well as noticing that her mother holds back from her.*]

Windy: And what is the consequence of doing that?

Carla: I don't think I'm letting mum know what I'm feeling and sometimes what I need from her and would like from her.

Windy: Yeah, and what do you think might happen if you were to do something different rather than continue to do the same and, I guess, get the same result from your mum, which is, for you, a disconnect?

[*Here I introduce the idea of doing something different as opposed to doing the same things and getting the same results.*]

Carla: Yeah. I think what I tend to do at the moment is go, 'Oh, I understand why she's like this,' and whatever, but it still feels like I'm not really getting what I would like or I'm not even having the courage to try something different out, maybe.

Windy: If you had the courage, what would you do differently?

[*When a volunteer, like Carla, says that they do not have the courage to try something different, I first ask them what they would do if they had the courage. Then, later I ask them if they could do that thing without courage. Also, sometimes as in Carla's case, I ask them what they mean by courage and work with their response.*]

Carla: I think I'd probably sit and say to her, 'I was on this Teams chat with Windy and the question came up of why don't I just say what I'm feeling, and I'd like to know a bit more about your inner world from time to time and sometimes I feel a disconnect,' and see what she does with that.

Windy: 'And, also, maybe I've been haunted by that 12-year-old experience of being really frightened about you killing yourself,' using suitable words, but, 'not wanting to upset you because of that'.

Carla: Yeah, and I think, when it happened, my grandad had just passed away, so I suppose that is resonating with me now, because dad with a similar sort of timescale. I can remember walking away from the surgery with mum just being quite frightened, but then trying to make her laugh or smile, if that would be the thing that would fix everything.

Windy: Right. But, in the same way, you're still trying to protect her from feeling hurt, aren't you?

Carla: Yeah, definitely.

Windy: You said that you would do it if you had courage.

Carla: ... [*Pause*] Courage.

Windy: What's your view of how courage develops, Carla?

Carla: Having a go, really. Getting a little bit outside of your comfort zone and... yeah. I think it was also around that time I started being quite OCD and quite a lot of rituals and things like that I developed.

Windy: Around which time?

Carla: Around about the age of 12.

Windy: Yeah. I guess it was your way of protecting yourself from pain, wasn't it?

Carla: Well, my mum's mum had died giving birth to her and then my grandad died and then I think, obviously, mum lost this one person and it was almost like there was a lot of death but nobody was really talking about it. And the way I was thinking, 'I can't have my mum or my dad pass away, so I'll unplug everything and come up with these kinds of weird rituals and prayers and things,' that I had to do.

Windy: Yeah.

Carla: And, when you say about it taking courage, there's almost this OCD controlling part of me that's frightened of... [*pause*] doing anything, because, in my own way, I've developed this protective bubble.

Windy: And the cost of that protective bubble is what?

Carla: If I say how she feels and then she does something, I might feel responsible.

[*I was aware of thinking that the issue of responsibility may have been a contributory issue but I was also aware that responding to this would have taken us away from the focus of how to connect rather than explaining reasons for the disconnect.*]

Windy: Yeah.

Carla: That's scary.

Windy: But, I guess, if you don't say how you feel, you end up not feeling connected.

Carla: Absolutely, and that's what I want. I really do....
                Yeah.

Windy: Do you know whether she still struggles with
                the same issues now that led her to want to...?

                *[I ask this question to see if there is still a
                reason for Carla to protect her mother.]*

Carla: ... I don't think she does. She's never spoken
                about it.... As far as I know, she goes to the
                doctor because she's got a bit of a blood
                pressure thing, but that's fine.

Windy: Yeah. Because what comes across to me, Carla,
                and it's understandable, that it's almost as if you
                haven't updated yourself or your mum in your
                mind.

                *[I introduce the idea that Carla may be
                operating on an outdated view of her mother.]*

Carla: No, I think you're probably right. I think you're
                right. I've always felt like I can't really say how
                I feel to her.

Windy: Yeah.

Carla: I've always felt that. I've always felt scared of
                talking about it with her.

Windy: But, in a way, talking about the fact that you are scared about talking about is talking about, if you follow my drift.

Carla: Yeah, yeah.... [*Pause*] My sister says to me, 'I just don't feel I know mummy,' and I say, 'No, that's how I feel sometimes.'

Windy: Yeah.

Carla: And I think about my relationship with my children and my family and my partner, it's not like that at all, and I'd like that or a bit more of that with mum.

Windy: Yeah. So, why don't you summarise, Carla, where we've got to at the moment?

Carla: I suppose I'm summarising, as you say, my outdated view; I'm still holding onto this from the past and it's very much impacting on the present, on the current. And... something about my courage and, perhaps, I don't know, thinking about... [*pause*] biting the bullet, really, in some sort of way.

Windy: Don't bite the bullet, Carla. You might break some teeth. The way I see courage is courage comes from doing things uncourageously.

Carla: Yeah.

Windy: Rather than having courage and then doing it.

Carla: It's an odd things for me because I feel like, in lots of ways, I am quite courageous and then in this way, in this particular relationship with my mum, I feel, yeah, that I'm not; I'm feeling protective and frightened.

Windy: Protective of whom?

Carla: Of her, I think, as well, and perhaps the child in me.... [*Long pause*] Maybe I'm worried that she will just – I don't know if she will reject me. I've never got that sense that she'll say, 'Look, I don't care,' or whatever. I've never ever got that sense, so I don't think that's the case.

Windy: I guess that one of the risks of trying to connect is disconnect, isn't it?

Carla: Yeah.... [*Pause*] Yeah.... Maybe I'm thinking I'd rather this than disconnect, I'd rather this than complete disconnect. Yeah.

Windy: Yeah, but I'm just wondering if the fear of disconnection is really based on – actually, based on what, because, in a way, you don't know your mother? In a way, what you do know about your mother is that it leads you to want to protect her. Leading to want to protect her leads you to feel disconnected from her.

Carla: Yeah.... Yeah.... Yeah.... I think I've got to mull that over a little bit.

Windy: Yeah?

Carla: Yeah.

Windy: Do you want to share what you need to mull over?

Carla: I suppose I'm not really understanding that as a concept or an idea, that I feel I need to connect her but I am disconnected, if that makes sense.

Windy: Well, you fear that, if you say these things and upset her, that somehow she'll push you away.

Carla: … [*Pause*] I think maybe I fear that, rather than pushing me away, there will be nothing more.

Windy: Yeah.

Carla: Yeah? I don't really fear she's going to push me away.

Windy: OK. But let's assume that. Are there other ways that you can connect with her?

          [*I am beginning to think that the session is not progressing. Hence the reason for this question.*]

Carla: I suppose… I've been trying to. I will go up and stay with her. Obviously, it's made it worse with Covid, but, after dad passed away, I was going to stay with her a couple of days a week, because I feel like, the more time I'm with her, the more chance... [*pause*] it might be helpful to spend more time with her on a one-to-one basis.

Windy: One of the things I went through in the lecture is that do you know what she wants from you? We know what you want from her, or for yourself and her, but do you know what she wants from you?

[*Since this is a relationship issue, I am once again bringing the other person into the frame by asking Carla what her mother wants from her.*]

Carla: I don't think I do and, if I talk to my sister about that, my sister doesn't think she knows. My sister's just had a stroke. My sister had a stroke just going into the lockdown. Mum didn't ring my sister at all and one day I rang up my mum and said, 'It would be really nice if you rang up Julie because she's a bit low and I think it will make her feel good if you were to ring up,' which she did.

Windy: Did she?

Carla: Yeah, and she did ring her up.

Windy: Maybe your mother needs some kind of prompt like that.

Carla: Yeah.

Windy: That it's not spontaneous.

Carla: I just don't think it is for her.

[*When Carla told me this about her mother it reminded me something about my mentor, Albert Ellis, which I shared with Carla.*]

Windy: I always tell the story about my mentor, Albert Ellis, who was somewhat on the Asperger's line. He was at a party with his then partner and the partner said to him, 'Albert, say hello.' 'Oh, OK, hello.' So, he had to be prompted to be social.

Carla: That really resonates with me, actually, because that's something that I've considered before. It's like, when mum came to stay with me last year for a week, a friend of hers was ringing her up on a daily basis to check she was OK, and I said to mum before we left, 'Do you need to let Yvonne know that you're going to be?' because she rang her up on the house phone; they don't have mobiles. 'You need to let Yvonne know.' And my mum said, 'Well, why would I need to let her know?' and I said, 'Well, she's ringing you up every day, mum. She'll be worrying about you, she'll be thinking about you. If you're not worrying, she'd worry,' and it hadn't occurred to her.

[*Here is what I was hoping for. The Ellis vignette resonated with Carla because like Ellis, her mother needs prompting to give a social response that she would not give left to her own devices.*]

Windy: And, when it occurred to her, what did she do?

Carla: She rang her straightaway.

Windy: Right. So, maybe that's your route in: maybe accepting that your mother needs some prompting in the same way as Albert Ellis did.

Carla: Yeah. Yeah. Yeah.... That makes a lot of sense. I think she does need prompting and maybe perhaps sometimes I'm expecting not to do so much prompting or I'd like to do less prompting.

Windy: Yeah, you would like her to do things more spontaneously.

Carla: Yeah.

Windy: And that's fine, but you have to ask yourself the question do you have a mother who is like that?

Carla: I don't think I do.

Windy: And, so, do you still want to connect with a mother who you may have to prompt to connect with you?

Carla: Yeah, I still want to connect with a mother that I might have to prompt to connect with me.

Windy: That may be the way forward. I don't know.

Carla: Yeah. Yeah. Yeah.

Windy: OK, let's bring this to a conclusion. Why don't you, again, do a bit of summary and particularly focusing on what you're going to be taking away, if anything, from our session together, Carla?

[As we are nearing the end, I ask Carla for another summary, focusing on what she will be taking away from the conversation.]

Carla: I think, in some ways, I'm taking away that stuff that I think I'd worked out a little bit myself: that mum seems to need a lot of prompting and that there was a part of me that was maybe thinking... that she didn't care or doesn't care, but, actually, I think she does. That was clear talking to you that she does care. So, I think I'm going to accept the fact that I'm the visitee and I have to visit mum for mum to show up, maybe.... Yeah... because she does show up when I do prompt her.

Windy: And, when she shows up, you may be able to talk about some of the things that we've spoken about today.

Carla: Yeah.

Windy: I don't know what kind of language she'd understand, but the idea is, in a way, it's summed up by the term metacommunication – talking about the difficulties of talking about things with her.

Carla: Yeah. Yeah. Yeah.... Yeah, I've got some ideas, because I know, if she watches something on the TV, when you talk about that you can sometimes bring....

Windy: So, that may be a way in. It's about understanding and accepting your mum as she is now, while understanding the fact that you're still, in some way, haunted by the person she was back then.

Carla: Yeah. I think I'm haunted by it because she doesn't really talk very much about stuff. So, you know when you say, 'I haven't had an update,' I don't feel like mum's updated me either.

Windy: No, but it doesn't mean that she can't.

Carla: No.

Windy: It doesn't mean that you can't find a way, particular, for her to update you.

Carla: Yeah.

Windy: But not spontaneously so; that she might need prompting to update you.

Carla: Yeah. Yeah.

Windy: OK. Is there anything else you want to bring up before we finish this evening, Carla?

Carla: No. No, I'd be quite happy to go off the spotlight now.

Windy: OK, thank you very much.

Carla: Thank you.

Windy: Thank you, Carla

> [*So, what Carla is taking away is that she needs to update her view of her mother and that her needs prompting to talk. After prompting her mother, Carla can use the opportunity to update her mother's view of her. Hopefully, the outcome of this process will be a greater connection between the two of them.*]

Carla's Reflections (20/4/21)

I started out being sceptical of single-session therapy, it was a great to be able to experience SST as a client and work on something personal. Its might also be helpful for readers to know I have worked as a CBT trainer for many years and recently qualified as a person centred counsellor.

My willingness to prompt my mum has completely changed, I had this idea of you do you and I do me, but was never quite sure how to navigate the space in which we collide. Which included do I have the right to prompt you or should I need to. Windy's Ellis anecdote really resonated with my experience of how my mum is and what he said about my need for spontaneity. I find myself looking back with a different lens, and more importantly my mum seems to like the prompting. It was recently my birthday, I message mum the day before asking her to call me at a given time the next evening. I got a lovely message back, saying that's helpful darling, I don't like to disturb you in case you're doing something, I'll ring you then.

6

Helping the Person to Accept the Cacophony of Feelings Towards Her Mother

Windy – Alison: Interview on 27/07/20
Time: 19 minutes 55 secs

Windy: OK, Alison, what relationship issue with your mother would you like to discuss with me this evening?

Alison: My mum and I have a dreadful relationship. I don't like my mother, and that's taken me a long term to say that and to be able to say that and not get really distressed over it. A lot of therapy has gone on there for that. But I think my mum didn't want me. She wanted me when I was a baby. I had two elder brothers and all I ever remember hearing was how wonderful my brothers were and I was always told, 'You're never going to amount to anything and you're not as good as your brothers and you never will be,' and I think I heard that message so much, what happened was I became that child. I have a younger sister and her experience was the same, but, obviously, I can't speak for her. But I grew up trying so very hard to please her and to please everybody, and then that came into adulthood. My mum's still alive. She's 94. And I have, through lockdown, made sure that I have gone every week, I've sat distancing in the garden, and I live the closest out of the siblings and nothing I do is good enough. She is horrible to me. She is spiteful and I really, really want to tell her. I want to tell her and I can't tell her, because I'm afraid to.

Windy: Right. So, what would you like to achieve by the end of the session, Alison?

[As usual, I ask Alison for her session goal at the outset.]

Alison: I'd like to be OK with knowing she's – I want her to say sorry to me for some things and apologise, and she's never going to do that, and I want to be closer to being OK with that, because, actually, this disturbs my sleep.

[As I discussed in my comments on my session with Grace – see Chapter 4 – wanting to feel OK about an adversity is problematic.]

Windy: Sorry, closer to being OK with what?

Alison: With the fact that she's never going to say she's sorry to me. She's never going to apologise. She's never going to be nice. She's actually never going to be the mother I wished I could have had, and I'd like to be a bit more OK with that.

Windy: And, by OK with it, what feelings would you experience that go along with OK?

Alison: I wouldn't feel eaten up on the inside, frustrated. I don't sleep well – sometimes it really, really interferes with my sleep. So, OK for me would be not having intrusive thoughts about her all the time, not devising ways that I'd like to torture her, which clearly I wouldn't do, but I do have the thought. I want to be OK in myself and let it go and just I think I need to be nice to myself. I don't know actually. I don't quite know how to get there, but I think I need to forgive her so I can move on, because she's going to die and then I'm worried I'm going to be left with this forever, because she's going to die sooner than later, isn't she, at 94? Yeah. So, that's kind of where I'm at.

Windy: Right. I'm still curious about what feelings you would experience. I know you said what you wouldn't experience, but what would you experience if you were OK and you forgave her for not being the mother?

Alison: I'd feel free, and free would feel light and... bouncy maybe, and I'm not going to say I'd feel happy, because I'm not really sure about the

word happy, but I'd feel OK and I'd feel light
and I'd feel a bit more bouncy and I'd sleep
better. Does that kind of answer what you're
asking me?

Windy: It does. I tell you my only concern – I'll be
interested to hear your views on it – is that you
still have what I call a very healthy desire for
her, even at this stage of life, to apologise to you
and say sorry. And, so, if we assume that you're
not going to get that from her, you're still going
to be left with a negative feeling, but I think it's
possible for you to have a negative feeling and
still being able to move on, whether it's towards
forgiveness or towards being OK with what's
going on. It's just that you wouldn't be getting
something which is important to you.

Alison: Yeah, and it bothers me it's so important. I just
want her to say, 'I'm really sorry, Ali, about…
the fact I made you feel like shit,' if I'm honest,
and I'm not going to get it, and, when my dad
was dying, when my father was dying – he died
of cancer, and so we had a good, healthy
conversation and I remember him apologising
and saying, 'Will you accept the apology from
me, Ali?' and I said, 'Well, I can accept it from
you, dad, I will, and thank you,' and he said,
'And on behalf of your mum?' and I said, 'Well,
I can't do that because she hasn't asked me,' and
he said the words, 'No, Ali, but your mum's not
very good at saying sorry and I don't think

you're ever going to get that.' And he said that
to me and I think that stuck with me.

Windy: OK, so, your father recognised that your mother
isn't good at saying sorry. Do you think she is
sorry?

Alison: No, not at all. She doesn't think that she did
anything wrong, when I have kind of alluded to
a couple of things that happened; she still, to this
day, will make the comments or blame me for it,
even though I was a youngster; I was a young
teenager. Yeah, she doesn't actually think she
did anything wrong. My mum was brought up
by nuns in not exactly an orphanage but in a
home, and so I excuse her because I kind of feel
that she wasn't shown very much love and
maybe wasn't taught how to love. So, I've
always used that as an excuse. But, if I'm really,
really honest, down inside, I feel I'm not being
congruent, because, actually, the honest truth is,
yeah, that's all well and good but it doesn't
totally flipping excuse her. And I've carried it
through my whole life.

Windy: So, if you were to be congruent with your mum
at this point in your life and her life, what would
that congruence look like and sound like and
feel like?

Alison: I think it would be... [*pause*] I worry that I
would start and not be able to stop. I worry that I

would say things to her that wouldn't be very nice. I worry that I wouldn't be able to just give her a little bit of it to test the water. I'd open my mouth and it'd be like throwing up in a bucket and the whole damn lot would come out. I'm not sure I would feel better about that. I think I might instantly, but, knowing me, afterwards that wouldn't sit very well, I don't think.

Windy: So, you fear that your congruence would be sort of spewing out of all your feelings about this and you, in a way, wouldn't want to do that.

Alison: Because I'm afraid of upsetting her, which makes no sense because I don't want to upset her but I live with the upset, and I'm worried she's going to die and then I'm going to be left with it even worse. I really worry about that. I think, 'God, if I can't do something somewhere to help myself now—'

Windy: OK. One of the things about congruence – I know it's not the same as the congruence that we learn about in counselling, but the congruence about the prepared statement, like they do in press releases: that you carefully craft something, which, in a way, is congruent to what you want to say, but without that sense that you're going to spill it out and vomit it all over her.

Alison: Do you mean the concept of like as if I was to write a letter saying exactly what I want to say, knowing she wouldn't necessarily see that letter? Is that the same concept? Is that what you mean?

Windy: That or something more direct to her that gives you a sense that you're talking to her, more from the point of what you've got to say rather than what she's going to say back. But maybe being mindful about how you would want to feel at the end of this process, a sense that, if you could say, 'Well, at least I told my mother how I felt in a controlled way, so I can then move on, even though I would ideally want the apology I'm not going to get.'

Alison: Yeah. I think, knowing how she is and the way she responds, because she's on me the minute I speak, I honestly think that anything I say—

Windy: Right. She wouldn't give you an opportunity to?

Alison: She will be down on me instantly. She does this, actually. She does the whole, 'Stop it! I don't want to talk about it.'

Windy: So, what that tells me is that you've got to come towards terms in this for yourself, intra-personally, isn't it?

[Up to now, I have been exploring with Alison the possibility an interpersonal solution to her problem with her mother. As a result of this exploration it is clear that such a solution is not viable and thus, we need to change focus and consider an intrapersonal solution.]

Alison: I think so.

Windy: What attitude do you think you could imagine having towards your mother that would allow you to walk away from this situation with sadness, because you're not getting what you want from her and sadness of the realisation that you didn't get the mother that would've been healthy for you, but that would lead you to move on and feel freer? What kind of attitude do you think that you would need to take?

[I suggest to Alison that such an intrapersonal solution would take the form of an attitude. In retrospect, I could have asked Alison what form she thought such a solution could take.]

Alison: Well, I think a forgiving one. I really try empathy, I do.... I've tried forgiving as well. Just I'm struggling with it.

Windy: What does forgiveness sound like, if you heard it out loud?

Alison: Not necessarily saying to her, but for me saying maybe out loud, 'Look, it's OK.' ... [*Pause*] What would forgiveness sound like? ... [*Pause*] Oh God. I kind of feel like bombarding. I've got all sorts of stuff going into my head now: what does forgiveness sound like? As I think it and think, 'Yeah, it's OK, mum,' a bit of me, there's another bit of me that says, 'No, it's bloody not.' So, actually, I'm struggling with it. I'm struggling with finding something.

Windy: OK, but maybe you need to include both of those parts in the forgiveness.

[*In reality, situations such as the one Alison is in involve the person grappling with different feelings towards the person with whom they have a problem. I mention this in the above response.*]

Alison: As in, 'You know what, it's not bloody OK, but actually it happened.' I can do that and I can either let it eat me up from the inside out or I can move on past it.

Windy: Yeah.

Alison: I do get stuck. I grasp the concept.

Windy: Get stuck at what point, Alison?

Alison: So, I'll say that and I'll think I'm thinking it and believing it, and I'll go to bed and get up the next morning, for example, and I've got to ring my mother and it's back again, churning away like a cauldron, and I think, 'Oh, OK.'

Windy: Sorry, what's back?

Alison: Just that. It's like a feeling of dread, really, or just... frustration, anger as well. It's all there. Because I have to have daily contact with her to check she's OK and that her carer's been and all this sort of stuff.

Windy: So, part of you fears her, right?

Alison: Oh yes.

Windy: Part of you is angry towards her.

Alison: Yeah.

Windy: And part of you forgives her.

Alison: Yeah. And part of me hates her.

Windy: Yeah, and part of you hates her. Right.

Alison: Yeah.

Windy: Now, the question is how can you bring this quartet of feelings together in some kind of harmony?

[*Alison is telling me that she has a variety of feelings towards her mother. In the time that I have with her, I cannot deal with all four emotions and to deal with one would not address her issue. This is the reason for the question above.*]

Alison: ... [*Long pause*] I don't know.... [*Pause*] You see, a bit of me thinks, if I could forgive myself, that would probably be a good start.

Windy: Forgive yourself for what, Alison?

Alison: Well, forgive myself for realising that that little girl tried very hard and, in fact, I hadn't done anything wrong. I just kept trying over and over and over to please her when, in fact, that wasn't what I needed to do. I was four or seven or whatever, and, actually, I just was a little girl, and, so, I didn't do anything wrong. And I wonder if I could forgive myself.

Windy: When you focused on that little girl—

Alison: Yeah. Say that again. Sorry, Windy.

Windy: When you focused on that little girl, who was desperate—

Alison: When I focus?

Windy: Yeah, when you focus on it, what would forgiveness sound like?

Alison: It would sound like, 'You know what, Ali, it wasn't your fault. You actually didn't do anything wrong. You're just as good as your brothers and you could be anything you wanted to be.' ... [*Pause*] I think it would sound like that.

Windy: Could I add a little bit?

Alison: Yeah, go ahead.

Windy: And your mother didn't have to recognise that. It would be nice if she had, but, for whatever reason, she didn't and, sadly, that was the way it was.

Alison: Yeah. She didn't know.

Windy: She didn't know what?

Alison: Well, maybe she didn't realise what she was doing and the effect it was having on me. She just behaved the way she behaved and didn't know, and still doesn't know – I don't think she does know that I've carried it for nearly 60 years.

Windy: Right. So, is it possible for you to forgive that 7-year-old in the context that we're talking about: that you're just as good as your brothers, but your mother didn't have to recognise that? You could be as good as them even though she didn't recognise that?

Alison: Yeah. I've never actually thought of that like that; that idea that she didn't have to recognise it. That's never been said... [*pause*] not something that had occurred to me. Yeah, I could.

   [*It is often a risk making a suggestion to a volunteer. However, it seems that my suggestion was something that Alison had not considered and could utilise.*]

Windy: Yeah, because, if she had to, then she would.

Alison: Yeah, and she didn't. But... yeah, maybe she just didn't have to do it in the first place. I just felt she did.

Windy: Yeah.

Alison: Yeah.

Windy: Are you a mother?

Alison: I am.

Windy: What kind of mother are you?

Alison: I'd like to hope, and I've tried to be everything my mother isn't to me.

Windy: That's what she taught you.

Alison: Yeah. I listen to him.

Windy: Do you know that?

Alison: Yes, I do now that.

Windy: That's what she's taught you. She's taught you how to be a good mother—

Alison: Yes, that's funny.

Windy: …. by being not a good mother.

Alison: Yeah, absolutely.

[I sometimes use this idea that our 'bad' parents teach us how to be 'good parents'. Alison seemed to resonate wit this idea.]

Windy: You learnt that lesson.

Alison: Yeah, he does. He says I'm great and he'll tell me anything. So, yeah.

Windy: Right.

Alison: And that is probably why I'm a product of that and I really set out deliberately to do that; to make sure I didn't.

Windy: Sure, yeah.

Alison: Yeah.

Windy: So, if we brings those things together: of you forgiving yourself as a seven-year-old for doing what a seven-year-old who was desperate for her mother's approval, even though you didn't have much of a chance of getting it, to recognise that she was the mother that she was and, sadly, that was the reality, and what she did teach you was the good mother that you are.

Alison: Yes.

Windy: If we were to bring those ideas together.

Alison: I like that, because, actually, that gives me that feeling that I mentioned to you earlier that I'd like: that lighter feeling.

[*Rather than ask Alison to summarise the points we have discussed, I enumerate them for her. She says that hearing it gives her a lighter feeling. Volunteers mentions have a lighter feeling when something shifts for them.*]

Windy: Yeah.

Alison: I had that lighter feeling when you said that to me about being a mother and she helped me be this mother, and that's quite interesting, because I actually got that light feeling that I'd said to you.

Windy: She didn't help you. You learnt what to do by doing the opposite.

Alison: Opposite, yeah. Yeah. Yeah. I do, on occasion, catch myself saying things and think, 'Oh my God, I sound like my mother,' but I'm sure everybody does that.

Windy: Yeah, I'm sure everybody does that.

Alison: I try not to.

Windy: You see, if you were to do that, then you'd come back and you can then say, 'Yeah, and part of me hates her and part of me is still scared of her.'

Alison: Yeah.

Windy: And it's OK to have this cacophony of feelings.

[*In retrospect I like this phrase 'cacophony of feelings' because I think it accurately describes what Alison is experiencing.*]

Alison: … [*Pause*] Yeah. Maybe I don't have to get rid of them.

Windy: No.

Alison: Maybe they can all just coexist.

Windy: Maybe they can coexist.

[*Alison takes up the idea and begins to think that her task is not to eliminate feelings and as she says they can coexist.*]

Alison: … [*Pause*] Yeah.

Windy: Because, in a way, isn't that what you're hoping for: that, at the last minute, your mother's going to say, 'I'm sorry,' and then that'll put an end to the cacophony of feelings?

Alison: Yeah, in an ideal world that would be nice.

Windy: Yeah.

Alison: But I know that's not going to happen.

Windy: It's times like this when I say, 'Good night, John boy.'

Alison: Yeah, 'Goodnight, Maryanne.' Yeah.

[*This is a reference to the end of 'The Waltons' where members of the Waltons family say goodnight to each other. It represents idyllic family life where all family members love one another. To be pedantic, Alison should have said 'Goodnight, Mary Ellen' not 'Goodnight Maryanne.' The main point is that she knows that we are referring to an ideal which in Alison's case was far from realistic.*]

Windy: OK. Do you want to just summarise where we've got to, what you're going to take forward?

Alison: Yeah. What I'm going to take forward, actually, is I'm alright. I'm OK and, actually, I don't have to forgive her and... I think I like the idea of it all coexisting. So, all those feelings, it's alright for me to hate her and I'm sure love her as well in a bit. She didn't realise, maybe didn't recognise what she needed to do and, because of that, I did recognise what I needed to do and how I needed to be as a mum. So, I really like that bit. That's given me that lovely feeling inside.

[*Having a volunteer end on a lovely feeling is a very good sign that some good work has been done.*]

Windy: OK.

Alison: That's good. I can go with that.

Windy: OK. Good. OK, thank you for sharing, Alison.

Alison: Yeah, thanks Windy. Thank you.

Windy: Thank you.

7

Helping the Person to Assert a Boundary with Her Father

Windy – Natalie: Interview on 09/10/20
Time: 20 minutes 51 secs

Windy: OK, Natalie, what's your understanding of the purpose of our discussion today?

Natalie: OK. Well, I know I don't have time to talk to you about everything that I could talk to you about, about difficult parents. So, I'm just going to pick one and today's going to be my relationship with my dad. I think… [*pause*] I'd really just like to talk about the relationship that I have with him, really, and maybe to come to, like I said before, an understanding maybe, an understanding really that we don't always get what we want and what we need and just the unhappy acceptance, I think.

Windy: Unhappy acceptance, did you say?

[*This appears to be Natalie's goal.*]

Natalie: I think so, yeah.

Windy: Yeah, OK. So, linked to what I was saying earlier, do you want to say a little bit about your difficulties with your father?

Natalie: Yeah. So, my parents divorced when I was about 10 years old. I'm an only child and we were an extremely close family and I was very much my daddy's girl – absolutely adored him, followed him everywhere, did everything with him. And he moved away and he still came to see me, was still very much a part of my life as I grew up and continued to do so, to be there, in and out of my life over the years. He's... [*pause*] not an easy person. He would say he's a very jovial person. He's a joker. He's actually a very difficult person to actually talk to, really, because he doesn't take anything seriously. I feel he doesn't take me seriously. He certainly doesn't treat me like a grownup. He calls me baby. I have just separated from my husband after 30 years of marriage and he is now checking on me three or four times a week to make sure that I'm OK. He's bringing me little treats, just like a little girl, bringing me little treats when he comes to see me. He doesn't listen to things I say. So, he frustrates me.

Windy: What have you tried to convey to him that he doesn't listen to?

Natalie: ... For example, these Zoom training sessions that we're taking part in, I always tell him when

I have one of those because I don't want to be disturbed. He obviously takes in the information but he doesn't listen or, if he does, he doesn't care, because he'll disturb me every time, almost every time.

Windy: By doing what?

Natalie: He'll come. He'll come to my house. He knocks on the window. He wants to be invited in. He wants my attention.

Windy: And how do you respond to him when he does that?

Natalie: I give in to him.

Windy: You do?

Natalie: I do, yeah.

Windy: And you want to continue to give in to him?

[Having heard a little of Natalie's story with her father, it appears that her problem here is that she 'gives in' to her father. I ask whether she wants to continue to do this going forward. This is, of course, an ironic question.]

Natalie: I've tried over the years, as I became... [*pause*] more grown, more adult and I felt more he's equal, adult to adult, I really started to stick up for myself and tell him, 'This behaviour isn't right, dad. You treat me like I'm your equal, really. You can't speak to me like this,' and what have you. We've been there. We've had such conversations and it's caused a lot of... unhappy conversations, but nothing....

Windy: Can I just ask you a question?

Natalie: Yeah.

Windy: What would he do if, for example, you told him that you had a Zoom event and to please not disturb you and you said to him, 'Look, if you do, I'm not going to respond to you'?

[In putting this to Natalie I am making a distinction between what she says to her father and what she is prepared to do with respect to him not interrupting her.]

Natalie: I think it would upset him.

Windy: Right. And you don't want to upset him?

Natalie: No, I don't want to upset him.... No. I'm mindful that he's getting older now.... *[Pause]* I think he's lonely. I think he wants my attention. He wants my company. So, I am mindful of that. But I also know that he's not respecting my need for privacy.

Windy: Yeah. Just on that point. You see, there's your dilemma: you want to be able to have an adult-to-adult conversation where he processes and takes into account and then acts on what you say, and that's not happening. The alternative is that, because he's not listening to your words, the only other alternative you have is for him to listen to your behaviour, and your behaviour is, 'Actually, I'm not answering.' You don't do that because either you feel sorry for him or you feel guilt or both. I don't know. So, there's your dilemma, isn't it?

Natalie: Yeah.

Windy: You want him to change but he doesn't listen and he doesn't take it seriously, being a joker, right, and yet the one way of getting through to him you're not prepared to do.

Natalie: ... No, because I don't want to hurt his feelings and I know what that feels like, because I think, well, I know he's hurt my feelings so much in the past.

Windy: So, if you didn't respond and you said to him, 'Look, dad, I am busy between 7 and 8:30, so, if you come, I'm not going to respond, but at 8:30 I'll let you in,' and so he might feel hurt if you don't respond, right? You're saying, 'Well, I know what that feels like and I don't want him to feel that.' I have a different perspective, if you're interested.

[*Natalie has a number of blocks to asserting a boundary with her father.*]

Natalie: OK.

Windy: Maybe the baby, baby, baby bit is him.

[*While Natalie has portrayed her father as 'babying' her, I put it to her that he is the baby.*]

Natalie: Yeah, I'm being the parent, aren't I?

Windy: It sounds like it.

Natalie: Yeah.

Windy: Maybe he needs to feel something bad in order to have a bit of a wakeup call.

Natalie: … Maybe, yeah. Maybe. He's pretty thick-skinned, though. So, maybe I just need to stick to my word.

Windy: Because otherwise you see what you're doing is you're saying to him, 'Look, please don't interrupt me between 7 and 8:30,' say, he interrupts you, you let him in, what are you teaching him?

Natalie: … [*Pause*] Well, he just gets away with it, doesn't he? He gets what he wants, gets his own way.

Windy: That's right, and he's also learning, 'Oh, I'm not going to listen to Natalie because she's not going to do anything. She'll let me in.'

[*I explain to Natalie that when she 'gives in' to her father she is teaching her not to pay attention to what she says because she does not keep to her word.*]

Natalie: Yeah. Yeah. I need to stand up. I need to stand up to him. At the age of 51 I need to stand up to my dad. Yeah. I mean, I have tried in the past and it's not been successful or it's been very unpleasant: there's been bad feeling and there's been a space of two years when we didn't speak.

Windy: Well, maybe small acorns need to be planted first. When's your next Zoom after this one?

Natalie: Ooh, probably next week.

Windy: OK. So, let me just outline a situation and see what you think about, based on what we're talking about, OK? You tell your father – and how do you do this? Do you do it by text or how do you have a conversation with him?

Natalie: Well, I'm sure I'll see him. He's going to pop in tomorrow morning.

Windy: OK. 'Look, dad, I'm going to be busy between 7 and 8:30. I'd really appreciate it if you didn't come round. Come round at 8:30, that would be great,' if that's OK for you, 'because it's important for me not to be interrupted, so I'm not going to answer you. Don't take that the wrong way but this is really important to me,' and you stick to that, right? And there's a part of you that's saying, 'Oh my God, my poor father's out there. Isn't it terrible,' and then you say, 'Now, wait a minute. Come on. Come on. Yeah, it's sad that he's upset, but is it so terrible?' and see what happens.

Natalie: Yeah. He's a grownup. I hope he'd be able to deal with it.

Windy: Well, if not, then you'll see, but at the moment you're not seeing, you're not discovering that because you're protecting him.

Natalie: Yeah.... Yeah.

Windy: And why do you think you're protecting him so much?

Natalie: … [*Pause*] I think that's what he's used to. It's what he wants.

Windy: What, your protection?

Natalie: Everyone's protection. It happened with my mum, it happened with his own parents, particularly his mother. Female protection, he loves it, craves it.

Windy: And, so, were he not to get it from you on this occasion, what's your prediction, just on this occasion?

Natalie: ... [*Pause*] I think he might be a little bit irritated, maybe, he's not got his own way, because he is used to having his own way.

Windy: Can you live with his irritation?

[*Natalie fears that her father will be very upset in the face of her asserting her boundary with him, but as we discuss it, it seems that he will be irritated something she can live with. In asserting the boundary, she is conveying to her father that she is not going to continue the female tradition of protecting her father.*]

Natalie: ... Yes.

Windy: Because the choice, it seems to me, is that you continue to play the role of the female for him, which is, 'Irritation, no, no', or, 'Now, wait a minute, he's sensitive but he's a big boy. He can cope with being irritated. Let's see what happens.' Do you think you might be prepared to do that experiment?

Natalie: Yeah, I think I do. Yeah.

Windy: Yeah?

Natalie: Yeah.

Windy: Do you have any doubts, reservations and objections to doing that?

Natalie: Oh no, not at all, but I'm not sure how successful I will be, but I think I'm going to have to do it more than once to be firm with him.

Windy: OK. Now, by successful, let's be clear about what you mean. What do you mean by success?

Natalie: He's not going to stay away. If he wants to come, he'll come, whether I tell him or not.

Windy: Has he got keys?

Natalie: No.

Windy: OK, so, he's banging away, banging away. He can't come down the chimney. He just can't get in. He's banging away because he's going to test it. He's going to test you.

Natalie: He will, literally.

Windy: He's going to be really saying, 'Right, these women are supposed to look after me. She's not hearing me. Bang, bang, bang, bang, bang, bang,' right? And you're saying, 'He ain't coming in. Why? Because it's not good for me and it's probably not good for him.' Bang, bang, bang, bang, bang, bang. I'm giving you the worst case scenario.

[I put this dramatically, but Natalie reports that her father will act like this.]

Natalie: It's going to happen. He does that. He literally does that.

Windy: So, is success you not opening the door until 8:30?

Natalie: Yes.... *[Pause]* Yes.

Windy: What would you have to think about the banging, in the face of the banging, in order to have that experience?

Natalie: ... *[Pause]* Well, it's very poor behaviour, really, on his part. So, it's quite immature, really. So, I can dismiss that. I can dismiss that. And..., yeah, maybe he'll listen to me next time when I say not to come because I'm not going to answer the door.

[*Note that Natalie's focus has shifted from her father being upset to his poor behaviour.*]

Windy: Because my hunch is you've got more chance of him listening to your behaviour that you have to your words, because his experience is that, 'The women in my life say one thing and don't stick to it and, therefore, I can get what I want and they're going to protect me.'

Natalie: Yeah.

Windy: I don't know him, but I'm just speculating. And you can say, 'Now, wait a minute, maybe there's a different way of doing this. Maybe I can hold down a boundary and keep to it and maybe he'll start to learn that there is a boundary there and that I'm going to stick to it.'

Natalie: Yeah.

Windy: It might be the beginning of something.

Natalie: Yeah. He's not fabulous with his own boundaries, so maybe I have to try.

Windy: You surprise me, Natalie! Of course he's not good with his own boundaries.

Natalie: Yeah.

Windy: Are you good with yours?

Natalie: … I haven't had a great teacher.

Windy: Well, you do. You know who you've got as a teacher? Natalie can teach Natalie to teach.

     [*In the absence of having a good role model, I put it to Natalie that she can be a good role model on this point for herself.*]

Natalie: Yeah. I'm getting an awful lot better, yeah.

Windy: Good. Are there times in your life that you've been successful, not necessarily with your father but with other people laying down boundaries with people?

Natalie: I set very good boundaries for my own children.

Windy: You do? Even though they might be upset?

Natalie: … [*Pause*] I hope so, yeah. I've always explained to them, if they are upset or they're not happy, I explain to them why the boundaries are there: that it keeps them safe. Yeah, definitely when they were younger they knew their boundaries, certainly.

Windy: And have they tried to test that in the past?

Natalie: As they've gotten older, yeah.

Windy: And what have you done when they've tested
              you?

Natalie: … Negotiated.

Windy: Right. And have there been times when
              negotiation didn't work and, therefore, you had
              to just say, 'No, that's the boundary and that's
              the way it is'?

Natalie: Yes. Yeah.

Windy: Yeah?

Natalie: Yeah, it's not always well accepted.

Windy: No. And how have you felt when it's not
              accepted?

Natalie: … If it's a boundary that's very important to me,
              then I think I feel that I have to keep that.

Windy: Right, even though your children might become
              upset?

Natalie: … Yes.

Windy: That's the Natalie who can teach the Natalie
              who I'm talking to.

              [I take Natalie's experience of asserting
              boundaries with her children and show her that

mother Natalie and teach daughter Natalie how to keep to a boundary with her father.]

Natalie: Yeah.

Windy: You've done it. You've got it in your repertoire. The question is how important is it to you to lay down this boundary with your father?

Natalie: It is. It's really important.

Windy: Then get in touch with that Natalie. Have a conversation with her. Learn from her.

Natalie: Yeah. It's been such a long time coming, Windy, it really has. Why's it taken me so long?

Windy: Well, I find that sometimes in my work I have to reintroduce a person with their past, in a way, and you've done it. All I'm saying is just revisit that, get that spirit, transfer it to laying down a boundary with somebody who looks like an adult, but, in certain areas – looks can be deceptive, Natalie?

Natalie: Definitely.

Windy: Alright. Do you want to summarise the work that we've done today?

Natalie: Yeah. I think, yes, I probably am more capable at setting boundaries and being firm with my dad probably than I realise, and to take more responsibility for the situation myself than expecting him to really follow the rules. He's not a great follower of rules, so maybe it's about re-education and maybe it's me who needs to do that rather than him.

Windy: Yeah.

Natalie: Yeah.

Windy: There's a song, an old Fifties song, it's called 'Keep a-Knockin' But You Can't Come In'.

Natalie: Absolutely.

Windy: Yeah.

Natalie: Yeah, I remember.

Windy: In brackets ('cos I ain't gonna let you in).

Natalie: Yeah. Yeah, maybe a 'Do Not Disturb' on my door.

Windy: You can say that as lovingly as you can, but, if your behaviour's not consistent with that, he's, 'You see, the women in my life aren't to be listened to because I can turn 'em.' Have you got what you came for?

Natalie: Yes. Thank you. I've left with a smile on my face. Thank you.

Windy: Good. Good. Excellent. Well, thank you very much, Natalie. Thank you.

[*As with Alison in Chapter 6, Natalie ends on a positive note which bodes well for the future.*]

Natalie's Reflections (09-05-21)

In my experience, single-session work helped me to focus on the problem at hand, without getting too caught up in the storytelling that often happens in therapy. But at the same time, I felt listened to and my feelings and emotions were all still noticed and recognised.

As a client, I would appreciate a follow up session on the work we did. I think this could be a valuable check in, to see if the initial session was useful etc, for reflection. Also this would be an ideal time to discuss if actions taken had then led to new issues or problems with communication with my Dad.

8

Helping the Person to Address Procrastination

Windy – Oscar Interview on 14/12/20
Time: 20 minutes 55 secs

Windy: OK, Oscar, what writing issue can I help you with this evening?

Oscar: Well, which one do you want? Oh Lord! So, I am at the end of my postgraduate diploma at Regents doing integrative psychotherapy and I have three essays outstanding: one on existential theory, another one on integrative theory and another process report. Now, the process report I think I've got a pretty good handle on, but it's the two academic essays that I find myself continually kicking into the long grass. Indeed, I've just received a second extension on one of them.

Windy: When were you given these assignments?

Oscar: Oh gosh, we're talking about the mists of time now. So, the existentialism one I believe was due for the summer, but we were then given an extension until December; and then the second integrative essay is due for around now – our term finished two weeks ago or something.

Windy: So, is it just you who was given the extension or was the whole cohort?

Oscar: Some of us had been given an extension. I'm aware that one of my colleagues, who may wish to remain nameless, is in fact on this same workshop, staring down the barrels of the same deadlines.

Windy: Yeah, OK. And so you applied for the extension?

Oscar: Yes.

Windy: OK. So, when is the new deadline?

Oscar: Well, technically speaking, two are due next week and the third one is due in March, but, because of Covid, we've been given an extension until the end of March, but it's not an extension that I can necessarily live by because I spend five days a week running a team in Brixton Prison as well as other things. So, I need to get on with it between now and the end of the year otherwise I'm going to be snookered.

Windy: And, so, what do you see the purpose of our conversation as being this evening?

Oscar: The purpose of our conversation is to get to a point of unblocking, really, because for one of these essays I knew all of this was homing into a looming cloud for some months and have done my dandiest to try and address it, but, as others have said in the chat, there's always a house to clean or a dog to walk or something to distract myself from.

Windy: And, so, which piece of work do you want to focus on this evening?

> [*In single-session work, it is important to create a focus for the session and this is particularly the case with people who procrastinate.*]

Oscar: Oh, which one? For the sake of argument, let's focus on this theoretical essay on existentialism, because that's the one that's going to be the latest.

Windy: Right. So, you've got a theoretical essay on existentialism.

Oscar: Yes.

Windy: How long?

Oscar: Three-and-a-half-thousand words.

Windy: Right, and how much have you done?

Oscar: None.

Windy: None. OK. And when's it got to be in by?

Oscar: The deadline was last Sunday but it's been extended, so ASAP, really.

Windy: ASAP.

Oscar: Let's call it the end of the year.

Windy: End of the year. So, we're on 14 December.

Oscar: My colleague, Julie, has just said 29 December.

Windy: OK, thank you. So, you've got 15 days to do it. OK. Now, how do you want to tackle this? Do you want to do words per day or how do you want to do it? What's your preferred way of working here?

               [*I ideally should have asked if Oscar was committed to doing the piece of work by the due date.*]

Oscar: I've always been someone who can only work unless he's under extreme pressure. I've tried in the past, including now, to pace myself through it and 'how do you eat an elephant? One bite at a time' type approach, but it's never really paid too many dividends. The last existential essay I wrote for this course I did in, I think two-and-a-half days and it ended up getting published in *The Journal of Existential Analysis*, so it wasn't a complete disaster.

Windy: So, you could say, for example, 'Well, my preferred way of working is to wait until the last minute, so I've got to hand this in on 29 December, so I will start work on this piece of work,' how many days?

Oscar: Christmas Day might be a good moment to give it a go. Christmas Day, Boxing Day.

Windy: OK. 'So, I've got four days to do this piece of work, so I will choose to start on 25 December because I prefer to work under pressure. So, by the 29th it will be done, so that will be it.'

Oscar: … Something like that.

Windy: Fine. So, what's wrong with that?

Oscar: I think, for me, what it is, is a frustration at the fact that I could better order my time. I'm perfectly capable in my job to not work to extreme deadlines. I'm perfectly capable, if a credit card bill comes flying through the front door, then I generally honour it on time. I just find, in academia, there's this longstanding procrastination block which I feel really holds me back in terms of, not only my life, but also my learning.

Windy: Well, what I'm actually saying to you, Oscar, is that, if you approached it in the way that you outlined to me – that you're a person who works best under pressure and that it's got to be done by the 29th and you're starting it on the 25th – you're not procrastinating. You're choosing to work in a particular way that suits you.

Oscar: … [Pause] That would be true if it wasn't the case that I was at a proclivity to just keep pushing the deadline back as far as I can. So, I've done more than my 100 hours. I've done almost 200 hours' worth of client-facing work.

Windy: But, if you knew, for example, that, if you didn't hand it in on the 29th, you wouldn't get your degree, would you still try to push it back?

Oscar: Well, yeah, I guess I would probably rise to that amount of pressure, but then I would probably just ask for another deadline.

Windy: Yeah.

Oscar: And that's what frustrates me: it's the fact that the deadline isn't that hard. I could announce, 'Oh, I'm off to Timbuktu for a year and I'm going to go and live with the Tuareg and I'm throwing my laptop out of the window,' and they'd say, 'Sure, have another year,' because that's the nature of the beast and why wouldn't I? I suppose I need to ask myself why I want to.

Windy: Presumably, they'll charge you an extra year's fees doing that, wouldn't they?

Oscar: I don't think so.

Windy: Oh, wouldn't they?

Oscar: No, I've paid for supervision and tuition. But you see what I mean? The original deadline was back in the summer when I was less busy, I was still on Covid hours at work.

Windy: So, first of all you seem to be saying, 'I work well under pressure and, therefore, if it's going to be on 29 December, then I could start work on the 25th and rely on my preferred way of working, my working under pressure, get it done on the 29th.' Now you're saying, 'Yeah, but I can always push it back.'

Oscar: Yes, that's the thing.

Windy: 'I can always push it back and, therefore, since I know that I can push it back and they will agree to my pushback, there's no point in actually starting work on the 25th.'

Oscar: That's it and it's the delayed suffering.

Windy: But what I'm saying is that you could existentially choose to do that.

Oscar: Yes, I could, and clearly I'm paralysed by my own freedom. I should probably write another essay on freedom and the poetry of T. S. Eliot or whatever.

Windy: Exactly.

Oscar: But I find myself in a place of just pray.

Windy: So, we've got two choices so far: one is for you to decide to start on the 25th, rely on your pressure-based hypothesis to get it done by the 29th. That's number one. Number two is, because you know that you can get away with another extension and that they'll wear it, that you won't start on the 25th. Are there any other options that you'd like to pursue with me at the moment?

Oscar: … Well, I guess those are final options that I have, really.

Windy: And which one do you want to choose?

Oscar: … Well, I would like to think that I'm going to honour this deadline, just to get the bloody thing out of the way.

Windy: So, you'd like to choose the starting on the 25th and handing it in on the 29th?

Oscar: I think so.

[Oscar's shows the slipperiness of the person with a procrastination problem. Even when I encourage him to choose latter option, note his response, 'I think so'.]

Windy: How do you think you might stop yourself from doing that?

Oscar: I think what I find myself getting into is what Steinbeck referred to as aligned perfection to get in the way of the good. So, thinking I can't possibly even begin to address this essay until I have the whole thing planned out to the letter in my mind and ready to just drop on the page.

Windy: Right, 'So, I have to write it in my head before I write it on the page.'

[My approach to dealing with problems of procrastination is to have the person specify the conditions that they think are necessary for them to start work on the project and then to help them to see that they could begin the task without these conditions being present.]

Oscar: Exactly.... In reality, what will happen is, it's a three-and-a-half-thousand word essay, I'll probably write 4,500, cut it about a bit, mix it up, have a look at the grammar, realise that I've forgotten most of the lessons that I learnt at school and pick it up from there.

Windy: Sure. So, the idea is that you believe that you have to have it mapped out in your head before you put it.

Oscar: Exactly.

Windy: Now, what do you think of that idea?

Oscar: I think it's clearly preposterous.

Windy: OK. So, you could choose for that to be coming into your mind but not to be guided by it.

Oscar: Yes, I guess so. I could get out of the way of that anxious thought.

Windy: Yeah. Recognising that, 'Yes, that would be my first port of call, I've got to have it in my mind, but, actually, no, I don't have to do that,' OK? 'I can actually approach it in a different way: a way that enables me to not put so much pressure on holding everything in mind.'

Oscar: Yes.

Windy: And, if you did that, would you then write it under those circumstances?

Oscar: I think I probably would and I think, also, if I lowered my expectations of myself.

Windy: What do you mean by that, Oscar?

Oscar: Well, I think what I mean is, is that I'm working towards more of a vocational qualification for which my academic transcript is not going to be necessarily leveraged to any great purpose beyond the initial proposition, which is to qualify for the BACP.

Windy: Well, OK, yeah, that's what I call pragmatic expectation: 'Well, you know, it's only a piece of work.'

Oscar: Yeah.

Windy: But what would you like to achieve for yourself on this essay?

Oscar: I think that's the thing: pragmatic expectation's got me sitting here talking about the fact that I haven't written a damn thing yet.

Windy: Yeah.

Oscar: I think what I would like to achieve, I would like to do give a good account of my academic and practical abilities. I wouldn't like to sell myself short. I mean, I could submit a passing essay at 50 marks, but I would probably be a little bit upset with myself.

Windy: No, if in the four days that you gave yourself you really recognised that you didn't have to hold all these things in mind and you actually spent the four days really trying to do it as close as you can do to what you would like to hand in, if you approached it like that, what do you think would happen?

Oscar: ... I think, realistically, I would probably manage to just about achieve what it is that I was looking to achieve. But, I suppose, in the world we're looking to try and minimise suffering, or at least in my life I am, and what I find myself experiencing is a tremendous degree of anxiety, self-doubt, suffering. You submit the damn thing and you think, 'Oh God, I've probably failed this one,' and then it comes back as a distinction.

Windy: Right, OK. But, because, while you're working to do it to the best of your ability, what is the suffering that you're going through as a result of that?

Oscar: I think it's the kind of crippling self-doubt more than anything else.

Windy: Meaning what? What does that mean?

Oscar: Like... an old submarine captain once said to me, 'The thing about courage is you don't know you've got it and you put the bucket down the well nine times out of 10 and then the 10th time you put it down, it doesn't come up wet and the other nine times don't count for anything,' and that's how I feel when it comes to these... fairly innocuous academic hurdles.

Windy: I'm not quite with you.

Oscar: So, what I'm saying is, is that, if my grade one average is distinction or whatever, then I can't rely on the fact that, 'OK, the prior five essays that I have written have been all distinctions and very well passed and great.' I can't say to myself, 'OK, Oscar, well, you were completely capable of doing that last time, so why can't you just sit your arse on this fairly indifferent office chair and just get on with it?'

Windy: You don't do that?

Oscar: No, I find myself wriggling around.

Windy: What do you do, in your mind?

Oscar: Well, as I say, cleaning, running.

Windy: Create the anxiety and the doubt, right?

Oscar: Yeah. I mean, John le Carré died today, so that's a good excuse to reread all of his oeuvre.

Windy: I know, but, again, that's an avoidance. But I'm saying what do you do to create the anxiety?

[*Note how difficult it is to get Oscar to focus on the salient issues. As is typical of the person with a procrastination problem, Oscar focuses on his avoidance.*]

Oscar: Oh, I think I probably conjure up images of failure in my mind: thinking, 'Oh God, I'm going to be inadequate and I'm not going to be able to.'

Windy: And what would convince you that that wasn't the case?

Oscar: Well, you would think the hard facts of my prior academic achievements, but apparently not.... I don't know.

Windy: So, what are you demanding of yourself, do you think?

Oscar: ... I think that's the thing, it's the demand, isn't it? I think there's a level of having to be a little bit more gentle with one's self.

Windy: Yeah. So, what are you demanding with yourself when you're anxious and crippled with self-doubt? You've done distinctions for the last five times, presumably you went through the same experience?

Oscar: Oh definitely, yeah.

Windy: You're now doing another one and right now you're crippled with self-doubt and anxiety. What are you demanding to create those feelings of self-doubt and anxiety?

[While Oscar does resonate to the idea that he is making a demand of himself that leads to anxiety and self-doubt and thence to procrastination, I struggle to have him focus on what is the nature of that demand.]

Oscar: … *[Pause]* I wish I had an easy answer.

Windy: Well, would you like to hear my easy answer?
[While it is best if Oscar identifies his own demand as he is struggling to do so, I ask him if he wants to hear my theory.]

Oscar: Yeah.

Windy: Well, I'm hearing, and I may be wrong, that you're demanding that you have to know that this one is going to be the same level and, because you don't know, then it probably won't be.

Oscar: Yeah. Yeah, I'm demanding certainty.

Windy: Yeah, you're demanding certainty that it will be a great piece of work while you're doing it and, because you can't convince yourself that it will be, then I think you have images and visions that it won't be.

Oscar: Yeah, and so you think, 'OK, well, why even bother trying?'

Windy: Yeah, exactly, and then you stop and then you rely on the generosity.

Oscar: A myriad of ways, yeah.

Windy: And, incidentally, I don't think that your institution's doing you any favours.

Oscar: Oh, none at all. Oh God no. I wish they'd turn around and say, 'Absolutely no way, Oscar. The trick's up. We're going to have you working on Christmas Day.'

Windy: But that's because they want you to take responsibility. Let's suppose that you went forward like this: 'I work best under pressure and, therefore, I'm going to start this on the 25th December and finish it on the 29th. I could extend it and I know that my institution would go along with that, but I'm going to choose not to do that,' right? 'I'm going to choose to do it on the 29th. Now, as I approach this, I have a sneaking suspicion that, first of all, my first tendency is to write it in my head first before I do it. I'm not going to go that route because that's putting a tremendous weight on my mind.

I also know that, when I get into this, I'm going to start off by being anxious and crippled with self-doubt because I'm demanding to know that this one is going to be a great piece of work and I don't know that it won't. Actually,' and this is the question you ask yourself, 'do I need to know that in order to do the work?'

Oscar: ... [*Pause*] And, immediately, you find yourself somatically just far more relaxed.

[*What I am doing here is bringing the two conditions that Oscar is insisting on before he begins to start work and to outline that he can choose to begin the task without these conditions being present. He responds by saying that this solution leads him to becoming more relaxed.*]

Windy: Yeah.

Oscar: That proposition: no, I don't need to know.

Windy: Exactly. 'So, let me work based on the idea that I seem to work best under pressure.' So, do you see what I'm doing? I'm trying to encourage you to build on your strengths but also to recognise that there are certain choices that you could take that would take you away from what you want to do and also ways of addressing your anxiety.

Oscar: Yeah.

Windy: Now, why don't you summarise the work that we've done and tell me what you think about it?

            [*Once again I ask the person to summarise the work we have done in the session.*]

Oscar: I'm not a CBT practitioner, I should say. I'm far more discursive. I think what we've done is, we've identified the pressure point, the stalling point, the circular and, perhaps, not very helpful narrative in my mind that tells me, 'You can't possibly do it because you're not guaranteed a success with this,' and that coupled with the fact that it's going to be some sort of crashing failure, puts me into a delaying mechanism if not procrastination, which is fundamentally working to a very hard deadline but really experiencing a huge amount of anxiety and anguish right up until the last possible moment whereby I know that, 'OK, give it three or four days and I'll probably be able to pull in something that will get a respectable mark.'

Windy: Yeah.

Oscar: And what I think you've inculcated in me is you've begun to fragment my binary thinking around that perfectionism and 'no, you don't have to be perfect, you can be good' type thing, which I think is East of Eden.

Windy: Well, and that you don't need to know which of those things is going to be while you're doing it.

Oscar: Exactly. Exactly. And just be in the process.

Windy: Right, yeah, to be in the process or you could suffer because, as a good existentialist, you might enjoy that kind of suffering, I don't know, and do what you've been doing. So, you do have a choice, which is, again, I would say, a good existentialist viewpoint.

Oscar: It is, indeed.

Windy: OK. Well, listen, I wish you well with that. It'll be interesting to see what happens by 29 December.

Oscar: Thank you very much, Windy. I appreciate your time.

Windy: Good, OK then.

Oscar: Thanks.

Windy: Bye.

Oscar: Bye-bye.

> [*It is in the nature of single-session work of this kind that I do not get to know the outcome of the session. At the very least, I have helped offer to*

see that there is a way he can tackle his procrastination problem if he chooses to do so.]

Oscar's Reflections (04-06-21)

Writing to you with a few minutes before your hard deadline despite being asked to make this slim contribution some weeks ago would, in my opinion, be indicative of the lasting efficacy of the session. Reflecting on our session, you made the situation apparent and clear to me in the moment, but I find myself yet sinking back into the old patterns of behaviour.

On a more positive note, the assignments were submitted on time and returned with favourable marks and comments from the examiners and with this brief note I honour my commitment to you, which you are free to use as you see fit. I think that a program of ongoing reinforcement would do me the world of good in this area of my life and I shall certainly consider approaching you as such (but perhaps not today!) Thank you for your support and precious – though I fear passing – insight into the nature of my ills.

9

Helping a Person to Integrate Different Parts of Herself

Windy – Emma: Interview on 29/06/20
Time: 13 minutes 59 secs

Emma: OK, has my microphone been turned on?

Windy: I can hear you, yeah.

Emma: OK, fantastic. OK, so... I guess mine is absolutely different from Anna. I'm in a state of – bringing in *Star Trek* here – I'm in a state of flux. I've had multiple losses recently: my husband died, I've moved countries, I've stopped working. I've lost my... reason for existence, I guess. My kids have left home and I'm struggling with how to move on. I guess that's it in a nutshell.

[Hearing this opening statement from Emma, a lot of counsellors would wonder what can be achieved in a brief session with her. In thinking this way, these counsellors would be adopting the conventional counselling mindset. By contrast, I am bringing the single-session

mindset which leads me to ask the following question.]

Windy: And, so, if you had that sense of taking the first few steps to move on after today's session, what would you have achieved?

Emma: I would restart my life again.

Windy: You'd restart your life again?

Emma: ... Yeah, because it's on hold at the moment.

Windy: OK. And is there anything that you can do to take it off of hold?

Emma: ... I know I could be more proactive, but I guess I'm kind of struggling with what I want to do, which, some of the time, is just kind of hide under the duvet and stay there and... [*pause*] I'm battling between that and actually doing something, whether it's letting new people into my life. It's re-finding my purpose in life, I guess.... [*Pause*] In old-fashioned terms, we'd say I just need a good kick up the arse... but I think I need some help in making that jump, in making that leap.

[Emma is divided, part of her wants to hide under the duvet and part of her feels as if she needs to be kick-started to doing something. One

of my goals in single-session work is to promote integration between divided parts of the self.]

Windy: OK. So, if somebody gave you a good kick up the arse, what would you do?

Emma: ... [*Pause*] I would run and go for things and try to be more proactive. I would be, perhaps, more open to relationships, but, on my personal life, it's early days: it's only 15 months since I lost my husband.... [*Pause*] I want to go back into private practice, but I'm in a different country with different rules and different everything, and it's trickier. And I'm very aware that what I'm doing is kind of leaving things until tomorrow. I'm not actually grabbing the reins and going with it. I'm delaying things, partly because of fear of what if I fail again? If it doesn't work, then what the hell goes on? ... What's the meaning of life when everything's gone?

[*I realise that in asking Emma the 'first steps' question concerning her goal for the session I was aligning myself with the part of her that wanted to get going. I pursued this here while being mindful of the need to promote integration between the divided self-parts.*]

Windy: So, it sounds like there are three things that you're kind of waiting for before you take a few steps: one is for somebody to give you a kick up the arse.

Emma: Yeah.

Windy: The other one is to have a guarantee you're not going to fail.

Emma: Which obviously there isn't.

Windy: And the third thing is that you want to find the meaning of life first before you move.

Emma: I'd put them altogether.

Windy: OK.

Emma: I don't know if they're in a particular order.

Windy: No. No. OK. So, are you waiting for those things to happen first before you take it off hold?

Emma: So, some days I'm just waiting for whatever to fall from the sky and fall in my lap. And other days I'm very proactive. So, it kind of depends on my mood. I've stopped sleeping, which doesn't help. My sleeping pattern is shot to pieces. So, in physical terms, I'm not really all there either.

Windy: Right.... And, so, it sounds like that there's a part of you that needs to be nurtured and a part of you that needs to have this sort of kick up the arse.

Emma: Yeah.

Windy: But you're not sleeping, you've had a grief. There's part of you that needs to look after yourself, but also there's an awareness that another part of yourself is actually wanting to go, and yet you've put all these kind of, 'No, I can't do that until these conditions are in place first.'

[*Emma is not sleeping. In my view, this, in part, may reflect the divided nature of her current experience so I give a voice to that part of her that needs to look after herself.*]

Emma: Kind of, yeah.

Windy: Now, I wonder if it's possible for you to move forward in that area of your life – we can come back and talk about you taking care of yourself in the other area of your life, but I'm wondering if it's possible for you to move forward in your life without the kick up the arse, without the guarantee that you're going to succeed and without the sense that you've got to have a meaning first rather than discover it later. I wonder if it's possible for you to do that.

Emma: And some days it is. I'm a great believer in the mantra: face your fears and do it anyway.

Windy: Yep.

Emma: And that's what I preach to others, and, at times, I do it, but I'm very aware that, at times, I really don't do it.... I go from superwoman to a little mouse in the corner, and I don't seem to be able to find the middle pathway, which is, I think, where I need to be, but I haven't found that yet.

Windy: So, you mean you want to bring those two parts of you together?

               [*This is not quite what Emma is saying. She is talking about finding a 'middle pathway'. However, I use this to bring in the idea of promoting integration between the divided parts of herself.*]

Emma: Yeah.

Windy: Supermouse.

               [*A humorous phrase which Emma likes.*]

Emma: I like it, yeah.

Windy: Yeah? So, what would happen if you were living a more integrated life without trying to kill either of those bits, what would life be like if you were more integrated in that sense?

Emma: It would be easier.

Windy: Yeah?

Emma: It would be more peaceful. It would be less stressful. It would be more productive.

Windy: Who's in charge of that integration, Emma?

Emma: Me.

Windy: You are? OK.

Emma: Yeah.

Windy: That's good.

Emma: I know it's down to me.

Windy: So, what steps can you take from our discussion today, perhaps, so that you can say, 'I've begun this process of integration'?

[*Here I keep the idea of beginning a process, but this time it is the process of integration rather than the first steps to be taken by the more active parts of her divided self.*]

Emma: … That's where I'm still struggling.... I suppose I would know what I would say to my clients, but I have a real case of physician, heal thyself.

Windy: What would you say to your clients?

Emma: I would say give it time and do things when it feels right for you, but I'm very impatient with myself....I don't have patience with myself. I'm very much, OK, I can tell everybody else what to do, but I need to be OK now, because, just to throw in it, in 48 hours I've had four people come to me: and this one's committed suicide, and this one's self-harming, and this one's just been diagnosed with lung cancer. And, so, I'm there for all of them, no problem, but I'm unable to give myself the same empathy and sympathy and loving and care that I can give to others.

Windy: Can I just clarify something with you? Are you saying that you're unable to or that you don't?

[I often ask for clarification when a client makes an important 'I'm unable to' comment. Are they unable or are they able but don't?]

Emma: OK, I don't. You're right, I don't.

Windy: Yeah?

Emma: Yeah.

Windy: And you'd like to?

Emma: ... [*Pause*] Yeah, I would.

Windy: So, can I invite you to speak aloud, Emma giving Emma some empathy and compassion at the moment?

> [*My sense is that Emma is struggling with self-empathy. That part of her needs a voice, so I invite her to give that part of her a voice.*]

Emma: ...

Windy: What would that sound like?

Emma: No, no, no, it would probably sound like, 'You know what, when you're ready to make those moves, you will make them. When you're able to make those changes and moves, you will be able to. So, stop stressing about it and stop pushing yourself.'

Windy: And how does it feel saying that out loud?

Emma: It actually makes me feel very tearful and emotional, because what it's showing me is that, actually, I'm being really hard on myself.

> [*The act of expressing a part of her that has not been heard is emotional for Emma.*]

Windy: And that what you really need to do is what?

Emma: ... Be kind to myself and go with me and not go with what I think me needs, if that makes sense.

Windy: Right, OK. The real you rather than some other version of you.

Emma: Yeah. So, actually, be congruent to what I'm feeling and not be what I think I need to be so that other people can see I'm OK.

[*Note the integrative nature of Emma's statement here, 'congruent to what I am feeling', precisely what she would promote in her clients. We also see the other-directed nature of the part of her that needs to be active. I could have focused on this but wanted to support Emma's integrative remark.*]

Windy: Right.

Emma: Yeah.... Maybe it's just I'm not ready yet.

Windy: 'I'm not ready yet'?

Emma: Yeah.

Windy: There was somebody called Ethelred the Unready. Maybe he had a wife called Emma the Unready.[3]

[*I find humour can be quite supportive in such situations*]

Emma: Yeah, it sounds like it could be.

---

[3] I called the volunteer 'Emma' because Ethelred's wife was named Emma of Normandy.

Windy: But don't forget you just said 'yet': 'I'm not ready yet.'

Emma: Well, I know I will be.

Windy: Yeah.

Emma: I know it will come.

Windy: And, so, maybe now is the time for you to be congruent, to looking after yourself, to recognise that this other part of you, this impatient part of you, will still be there, but you have a choice about whether to be guided by that part.

Emma: Yeah. Yeah, I guess.

Windy: Or to be guided by the part of you that is a bit scared and needing some empathy and some self-compassion and to take your time.

Emma: Yeah.

Windy: And it's a question of choice about which part of you that you could be guided by.

Emma: Yeah, and I do go with superwoman because, obviously, I can cope with and do everything... but that's not really where I'm at.

Windy: Right. Where are you at?

Emma: I still want to be the mouse in the corner and I want to be looked after and I want to be nurtured. And, if there's nobody else to do it, I have to do it for myself.

Windy: So, what kinds of things can you do to nurture yourself and look after yourself?

Emma: I guess the first step is actually acknowledging that I'm not ready to be superwoman yet.

Windy: Would you like to make a public announcement to three hundred people to that effect?

Emma: Four hundred, but, yeah, I'm not ready to be superwoman yet.

Windy: I'm sorry, I didn't quite catch that. What did you say?

            [*I use what I call the 'deaf old man' technique to encourage a person to say something important with emphasis.*]

Emma: I'm not ready for that yet. I'm still in the process and I still have to be me. I have to be more congruent and more empathic to myself.

Windy: Right.

Emma: Which I haven't been.

Windy: Right.

Emma: … Yeah. I need to listen to my inside and not my head…. And it's about connecting the two. I'm very good at working with one. I'm very good with working with the other. But what I don't have is the straw that connects them.

Windy: You don't have or you don't use?

   [*This is a similar intervention similar I made earlier concerning 'inability vs. ability + don't'. There is a difference between not having a skills as oppose to having a skill and not using it.*]

Emma: Yeah, I guess it's there in the cupboard. I just need to take it out of the cupboard and use it.

Windy: OK. So, if you took it out of the cupboard and used it, how would you know you were doing that?

Emma: Because I'd be a hell of a lot kinder to myself.

Windy: Yeah?

Emma: I would have fewer expectations of myself… [*pause*] and I would listen to my heart or my soul or whatever we want to call it and not to the brain that says, 'Yeah, you know, you need to get together because you've got to buy food next week.'

Windy: I guess that other part of you is still going to try to grab your attention, isn't it?

Emma: Yeah, but it's a matter of being aware of it and saying, 'Yeah, OK, there's a time and place for you, but it's not yet.

Windy: Right. Could you just do what you did with your hands again?

Emma: What, this?

Windy: Yeah. Well, maybe that's important. Could you do that again? How does it feel to do that?

[Sometimes a person will do something non-verbally that expresses an important feeling. I noticed Emma making a hand movement and asked her to do it again and to voice the feeling that she has when she does so.]

Emma: It's actually quite... *[pause]* – what's the word? It feels like a release. It's like letting the pressure out of a boiler or a tap when you turn it on. It's letting things go.

[In single sessions, when there is a shift for the client they talk about some kind of release or feeling lighter.]

Windy: Maybe you need to remember that, to do that in response to some other urgings from a different part of you.

Emma: Yeah.

Windy: Part of the response.

Emma: Yeah.

Windy: Thank you. Is there anything else you want to add to that?

Emma: No. I think I've thrown enough at you already.

Windy: OK. Well, thank you very much.

Emma: Thank you. That was wonderful. Thank you.

Windy: Let's stop there. Thank you.

> *[Note that I did not ask Emma to summarise the work we did together. I did not do so because I wanted her to go away with the physical release that she experienced at the very end. Anyway, I was sure that she was going to takeaway the importance of being congruent with her feelings as the integration she needed.]*

Emma's Reflections (03-06-21)

As far as the session was for me – I found it to be transformative. You managed to hone in on my words, and feed them back to me in a way that made me think on a deeper level about them and actually feel the REAL underlying emotions and thoughts rather than just the superficial ones.

The skill of enabling such a process in such a short space of time is truly amazing, and one that I would love to delve deeper into and discover for myself!

I am used to working therapeutically in a medium to long term basis, and so do actually experience the effect of single-session therapy was astounding. I can only thank you!!

10

Developing a Plan for the Person to Accept Herself in Birmingham

Windy – Agnes Interview on 22/02/21
Time: 21 minutes 56 secs

Windy: Thank you for volunteering this evening, Agnes. What's your understanding of the purpose of our conversation today?

Agnes: My understanding is, yeah, just to get a bit of clarity, really, about the feeling of shame, and my experience is a bit more general and long term than Daphne's, so I'll be interested to see how that works in a single session.

[Daphne had been the previous volunteer that evening.]

Windy: OK. And, if you had that insight, would you want to do anything with it?

[Agnes's session goal is a little vague so I use her wish for clarity or insight as a process goal and see it I can link it with an outcome goal.]

173

Agnes: … Yes. I'd like to change some behaviours that I've got. Yeah.

Windy: OK. Would you think it's more helpful to talk about your experience of shame first or the behaviours that you would like to change?

Agnes: Probably the context around it. So, the basis of shame. I hadn't actually planned to volunteer until I just saw the chat and there was a lot of chat around religion and that really sparked something for me, because that was my experience.

Windy: OK. So, could you help me to explain the context?

Agnes: Yeah. So, I was raised in a cult and, when I say cult, it wasn't anything too weird. It was roughly based around Christianity, but we were also worshipping somebody as well as the religion. There was one person who was in charge of this whole setup and was really controlling. I don't know any different. My mum joined this cult when I was two years old and I managed to escape when I was about 16. So, it was all my formative years, my early development and, yeah, even though that was a long time ago, and I've done a lot of work around it – so, I'm only a trainee therapist, but I've done a lot of work in personal therapy around it and I've got a lot of understanding around the general concepts of religion and indoctrination and things like that. But, as I say, it does still... influence my behaviours, especially my relationship with my mum and how I behave around her; I go back to my 10-, 12-year-old self when I'm with her.

Windy: Yeah, as we all do. I used to go back to my 10 and 12 self when I was 60 with my mother. Is your mother still within the cult?

[My goal here was to 'normalise' this phenomenon, but I am not happy with this comment because I made it before fully understanding Agnes's experience.]

Agnes: She's not, no. She was treated really badly, actually, and she was sectioned as a result, and she was since diagnosed with schizophrenia. Yeah, she had... almost a much worse time. She was in it for a lot longer than me and she had a bad experience. And, so, luckily, that was enough for her to remove herself from it, but she's had her own issues trying to recover from it as well.

Windy: Sure.

Agnes: And the two things have affected our relationship quite a lot.

Windy: So, when do your feelings of shame come to the surface in terms of your experience?

Agnes: So, it's evolved over the years. So, when I immediately left, it was around sex and relationships and the guilt of all that kind of thing. Then that's kind of waned now that I'm married and a bit older. And then it morphed into something else. At the moment, as I say, it seems to be – I've established myself away, physically away from where that all happened, I've got my own life now, but it's whenever I go back to Birmingham – and I nearly said 'luckily', that was interesting – that's not been a while with lockdown, but, whenever I go back, I get this incredibly feeling of shame.

Windy: In Birmingham?

Agnes: Yeah.

Windy: So, it's something to do with the location.

Agnes: Well, that's where the church was, that's where my mum still is, so it's got a lot of memories.

   [*The location becomes important later on.*]

Windy: It's interesting that you almost see your feelings as morphing from one experience to another. But I'm just wondering what would be, for you, the language of shame in terms of your judgments about yourself, when you feel those feelings?

[The subject of my presentation earlier in the evening was on SST and shame. I made the point in that presentation that it is important for the therapist to work with the client's shame-related language.]

Agnes: ... That's a good question.... *[Pause]* Yeah, just that feeling of disappointment that you said, it's kind of morphing into that a little bit, but just feeling that I'm a disappointment, because, even though my mum's left that particular cult, she's still very religious and I've gone completely the other way, more into atheism. So, I just feel that I'm this huge disappointment and I'm a heathen, I'm a sinner.

Windy: So, it's related to your inference that you're a disappointment to your mother. Is that what you're saying?

[As you can see there are three elements expressed by Agnes, 'I'm a huge disappointment to my mother', 'I'm a heathen' and 'I'm a sinner.' I went with 'I'm a disappointment' whereas I should have ideally asked here which one of these identity statements resonated most with her experience of shame. Also, I edited out the term 'huge' which was an error as the omission minimises Agnes's experience of shame.]

Agnes: Yeah.

Windy: Have you checked that out with her?

Agnes: Yeah.

Windy: And what did she say?

Agnes: Well, again, it's changed over the years. At first, she was very disappointed and I wasn't taking the route that she wanted and she could see all the mistakes I was making, but then the more ill she became mentally, the more the roles reversed. And with age as well, she's becoming elderly now, I'm nearly 40, so there's that shift anyway. But, yeah, when I've talked about it recently, probably about three years ago was the most recent when we had that discussion, she always says, 'Absolutely not. I'm very proud of you. You've turned out really well.'

Windy: So, what gives you the sense that you're a disappointment to her?

Agnes: It's probably just... [*pause*] I feel like it's not updated in my head. That's how I used to feel and, as I say, whenever I'm in her presence, I feel 12, 14 and that's exactly how I felt then; that I was a disappointment. So, it's almost as though that bit's stuck and that, OK, I'm older and that's no longer relevant.

Windy: What's no longer relevant?

Agnes: That feeling of shame; that I'm a disappointment.

Windy: Well, it's relevant in the sense that you experience it, isn't it?

[*In retrospect, I am not sure that my questions about whether or not her mother did regard her as a huge disappointment were that useful, but I do bring things back to Agnes's experience of being a disappointment which is. Of course, the most relevant point.*]

Agnes: Yeah. Yeah.

Windy: There are a number of routes that we could take. I am just wondering what you might find useful. I know you mentioned behaviour which I'm still yet to understand, but do you think it would be useful if I helped you to look at your own self-judgment in the face of being disappointing your mother?

[*While, I mention a number of routes, I really only outline one here although I do make reference to Agnes's behaviour.*]

Agnes: Yeah.

Windy: Do you think that might be a useful thing to do?

Agnes: Yeah.

Windy: Do you think it's possible for you to be a disappointment to your mother and not to be a disappointment to yourself?

             [*My way of working with shame is helping a person to see that self-acceptance in the face of other-rejection is therapeutic and useful because the self-acceptance part is under the person' control.*]

Agnes: ... Yes, yeah, and... I have shifted a little bit. I'm not quite where I want to be.

Windy: I mean at the same time.

Agnes: ... Yeah, holding those two things together?

Windy: Yeah.

Agnes: In theory, yes.

Windy: In theory?

Agnes: In theory.

Windy: How would it sound in theory?

Agnes: Well, I do believe you can hold two things like that together, but I've just not experienced it and it's been so long and I feel like everything is so ingrained that it seems... [*pause*] almost impossible.

Windy: Which bit is almost impossible?

Agnes: To hold them. To not feel disappointed with myself but to feel like a disappointment to her.

Windy: So, it's difficult for you to conceive of you, in a sense, accepting yourself in face of your mother's non-acceptance of you?

Agnes: … Yes, yeah.

Windy: OK. But are you saying you haven't tried that?

Agnes: No, I have. I have. And, as I say, I feel like there's been a shift, because I was quite unwell in my 20s mentally. It really used to affect me and I used to do everything to try and gain that approval. The percentages have shifted, so now I'm 80 per cent comfortable with myself, whereas before I was 10 per cent comfortable with myself. But I don't see 100 per cent as being attainable.

   [Agnes has worked on the issue of self-acceptance and has made progress but there is an element missing as we will see.]

Windy: 100 per cent comfortable in yourself?

Agnes: Yeah. So, it's bearable. 80 per cent is bearable and I can get on with it.

Windy: I often use the words 'working towards'
          unconditional self-acceptance, because it's a bit
          like self-actualisation: you never actually get
          there. I'm just curious about whether it's worth
          us talking about how to utilise that idea that you
          can still focus and be disappointed, in a way,
          that you're a disappointment to your mother as
          your 14-year-old self. I'm wondering if it's worth
          you processing that information by your 14-year-
          old self, if you can access that part of you.

          [*Given the fact that Agnes needs to process self-
          acceptance more experientially, I first introduce
          the idea of doing so as her 14 year-old self*]

Agnes: … How would I do that?

Windy: Well, can you imagine your 14-year-old self?

Agnes: Well, I can, but it seems like… [*pause*], well, it
          is a memory, but it doesn't feel very realistic.
          When I think of myself as 14, it's just I feel
          quite removed. I think I've detached myself
          slightly. It was all so painful.

Windy: Yeah. I'm not necessarily going to suggest that
          we do that now, but it sounds like that might be
          something, because I think that you're able to
          process the idea, at least theoretically, that it's
          possible for you to accept yourself in the face of
          your mother's disappointment. I just think you

need to do that in Birmingham, because you're not in Birmingham now, are you?

[*This is the other element of experiential processing of self-acceptance. Agnes needs to do this in the place where she experiences her feelings of shame – Birmingham.*]

Agnes: Exactly. I feel a lot better when I'm physically removed from the situation.

Windy: Yeah, and what I'm suggesting is that you may need to, by taking care of yourself, but maybe to do that work in Birmingham, because, when you're in therapy, are you in therapy in Birmingham?

Agnes: No.

Windy: So, I think the location is really quite important.

Agnes: OK.

Windy: Have you ever thought about that before?

Agnes: I've always known that the location is important because I would absolutely dread going to Birmingham for about a week before the train was booked or something, and then I would try and do things in Birmingham that were enjoyable to try and re-shift things. I don't think

I've really tackled it head on. It's always been a bit of a distraction thing.

Windy: Yeah, and, as I say, we're not going to be able to do that tonight, but I think the thing I would wonder about is the therapeutic potency of actually doing that work so that it actually becomes more experiential.

[It has become crystal clear that Agnes and I are not going to be able to do the experiential work that she needs to do in a single session and certainly not in front of a large online audience. Consequently, I shift to helping her to develop a plan to do this work in Birmingham as we will see. When the therapeutic work that a client needs to do exceeds what can be done in a single session, then I will shift to talking about what they need to do after the session going forward.]

Agnes: Yeah.

Windy: And that you can actually start that work at the time when you are planning to go to Birmingham, because it sounds like that kicks in as well. And I think, when you're not going to Birmingham and you're not planning to go to Birmingham, I think that that emotionality is not there for you and I think that it sounds like that more intellectual processing.

Agnes: Yeah.

Windy: Look, I'm not knocking the intellectual processing, because I think that that's important. I don't think it's sufficient.

Agnes: Right.

Windy: But I do think that you need to do that. I often have a concept which I call 'challenging but not overwhelming' when I'm helping people to do that kind of work; in a way that you need the challenge of Birmingham without being overwhelmed by it or, if you are overwhelmed, you can actually bring it back to the challenge.

   [I use the concept of 'challenging but not overwhelming' a lot in my work. Without a degree of challenge the work will be theoretical and thus, lacking therapeutic potency, however if the client is overwhelmed, processing will shut down and there is the potential of harm.]

Agnes: … Yeah.

Windy: What do you think of that idea?

Agnes: Yeah. I'm not quite sure what that would look like, but, yeah, I agree with the concept.

Windy: Is it worth talking about the behaviour that you mentioned? You spoke about behaviour that's related to the shame.

Agnes: ... Yeah.... [*Pause*] I'm not really sure how to describe it, but, like I say, it's almost like a regression to my younger self. So, I am quite argumentative around my mum, quite hostile almost, ready for a battle.

Windy: And how do you feel about the way you are behaving, when you behave that way?

Agnes: ... How do I feel about it? ... I almost feel like I don't really have a choice, because, if I just go in... normally... it's almost like a learned behaviour – being myself didn't really work in the past, so I have to put this armour on and go into battle in Birmingham.

              [*Agnes's behaviour seems self-protective.*]

Windy: Right, OK, yeah.

Agnes: Yeah, I'm not thrilled about it, but it kind of feels necessary.

Windy: And what would happen if you didn't do that, if you didn't put the armour on and you didn't go and fight?

Agnes: I'd just feel like I'd get trampled somehow.

Windy: Trampled in what way?

Agnes: … [*Long pause*] I don't really know.

Windy: Is there an image that goes along with that trampling?

Agnes: … Almost like in a riot, just being flattened by… horses and people.

Windy: And what happens then?

Agnes: I just get flattened?

Windy: And what happens then?

Agnes: I can't get up again.

Windy: For how long?

Agnes: … [*Pause*] Quite a while, until I—

Windy: Until you?

Agnes: My legs might be broken or I can't physically get back up again and that I'd require medical attention, I don't know. This analogy's running away with me.

Windy: But it actually feels that physical, doesn't it?

Agnes: Yeah.

Windy: That somehow you're not just being emotionally trampled on, you're being physically trampled on. Then, if you feel that, it makes perfect sense to go in with your armour.

Agnes: Yeah.

[As can be seen from Agnes's response, the imagery that she has concerning what will happen to her if she does not put her armour on contains both emotional and physical harm. I make the point that in this circumstance putting her armour on makes perfect sense.]

Windy: As I say, we're not going to do anything about that, but I'm just wondering if you could allow yourself to go back to Birmingham and be that protective self whenever you're there, and to drop it when you feel able to drop it, but to have it, because it sounds like it is a protective part of you.

[The plan to do the self-acceptance work given what Agnes has said about what she fears happening to her without her armour features the importance of Agnes being self-protective.]

Agnes: Yeah. I think that would be the key bit, the control over it, because in the past I've had panic attacks, I've had all sorts of bad reactions to being there and trying to tackle things and bring things up with my mum, and I think pre-emptying things has never gone very well. So, perhaps just, yeah, not putting too much pressure on it and, if the moment arises and I feel strong and comfortable, then perhaps do something then.

Windy: Sure. This is going to sound actually bizarre, but, in terms of what I was saying about challenging but not overwhelming, it's probably not going to be possible pragmatically, but it's almost as if I'm recommending that, if you're going to go back in therapy, you first start off with somebody on the outskirts of Birmingham and then you gradually work yourself towards the part that you need to do the work in but you've got the support with you.

Agnes: Yeah.

Windy: It's kind of weird. I don't know if that makes sense to you, because it sounds like that's what you're doing for yourself: you're saying, 'Look, I need protection, I need support and, if there's nobody there to do it for me, I'm going to go in there with my armour.' So, that's why I'm saying, in a funny kind of way, that work does need to be where the pain is but the pain's got to be dealt with in a controlled way.

[Although my suggestion is not plausible, I made it to convey the point that the work that Agnes

> *needs to do needs to be gradual and geographically relevant.*]

Agnes: Yeah.

Windy: OK, so, do you want to summarise the work that we've done today?

> [*I have made the point that having the client summarise at the end is an important part of single-session work. Here it is also important in that it enables Agnes to get closure from the distressing material she has been discussing in the online space.*]

Agnes: ... So, I've been talking about a long-term feeling of shame around breaking away from a religion and how that's impacted my relationship and looking at how I can feel better about that, really, and tackle it and try and... get some peace around it and feel confident with myself despite disapproval from others.

Windy: And is there anything that we've discussed that you might be able to implement?

Agnes: Yeah, I definitely like the CBT approach of the gradual – I can't remember the name of it, but the working my way up to it. I think I've always overwhelmed myself with it.

Windy: Yeah.

Agnes: And, like you say, it's not 'will I ever get there, will I ever be 100 per cent' – probably not, but I can make progress, I can make... inroads into it.

Windy: Yeah, and you could do that while protecting yourself.

Agnes: Yeah.

Windy: And maybe drop it if you feel more comfortable about doing that.

Agnes: Yeah.

Windy: Well, let's see what the group think. Thanks for discussing it with me.

Agnes: Thank you.

[*I think that Agnes has taken away something of value concerning any future work that she decides to do on her feelings of shame concerning visiting her mother and visiting Birmingham.*]

Agnes's Reflections (26/04/21)

I knew of Windy's work from my studies as a current counselling student and have always been curious about the idea of single-session therapy. It was for this reason, rather than the subject matter itself, that led me to sign up for the talk. When it was mentioned at the start of the talk that volunteers would be asked for the second half of the talk, I didn't pay much attention. I am a fairly introverted person and speaking in front of other people has never really appealed. However, the more I heard Windy talk about shame, the more the cogs in my head begin to whirl. Amidst all the chat amongst the other attendees, there were comments on shame and religion, and this really resonated. My experience with religion has been extremely negative and my former years extremely damaging. It is what led me to counselling, and, in many ways, counselling training. But I hadn't thought about it so much through the lens of shame. I suddenly found myself wanting to explore these feelings further and found myself volunteering.

When I was chosen, I felt a surge of adrenaline. As I say, I am not a fan of public speaking, but the online platform helped me to forget about that. My experience of single-session therapy was interesting. I liked the fast pace of it and the directive questioning. It was interesting to see that Windy honed in on the physical location of my trauma – Birmingham. I knew that this was a factor due to my feelings whenever I return there, but it was interesting to see how this developed, with the idea of gradual exposure and even potentially doing some counselling in Birmingham. I haven't done this yet and not sure I will, but it made me think. Especially as I am just making plans for my next visit and experiencing the familiar anxiety of doing so.

Windy recognised that this was not going to be resolved in this one session and I agree. But it definitely gave me some food for thought. As a trainee counsellor I really enjoyed reading about Windy's thought processes in the transcript after the event as it was really helpful to discover what he felt was effective and how that measured up to my experience as the client.

Overall, a really thought provoking and stimulating experience for which I am grateful to have been involved in.

11

Helping the Person to Address Performance Anxiety

Windy – Carolyn Interview on 29/03/21
Time: 21 minutes 1 sec

Windy: Hi Carolyn, what's your understanding of the purpose of our conversation this evening?

Carolyn: My understanding really is to look at my issue around anxiety and to hopefully come away with something that's going to help me moving forward with my issues around it, really.

Windy: OK. How would you describe your issue with anxiety?

Carolyn: It's quite specific. It's to do with if I was to deliver a presentation to a group of people.... I've got it now while I'm speaking to you because I'm aware there are a lot of people who will probably be watching this as well. So, it's been a real challenge for me to actually volunteer and do this.

Windy: How did you get yourself to do that then?

[*Whenever a person wishes to discuss a problem and by volunteering that they are taking steps to deal with the problem, it is important to help them to understand what they are doing to take these steps.*]

Carolyn: Well, it's something that I'm working towards anyway, so this is perhaps another element of a test to myself to build that evidence up, to show that maybe it's not as bad as I think. It's not so bad at the moment because, although I'm aware people can see me, I can't see people looking at me.

Windy: Right. And, so, if you could see them, would that make a difference to you?

[*I missed a chance to show Carolyn that her attitude – 'it's not as bad as I think' – played an important role here. Instead, I pick up on the aspect of the situation that has made it easier for her – she can't see people looking at her.*]

Carolyn: Yeah.

Windy: OK. That's helpful. So, what would you like to achieve by the end of the session?

[*Once again I ask the person for their goal for the session.*]

Carolyn: I'd like to come away with perhaps not feeling quite so fearful about talking in front of a group of people.

Windy: And have you got something coming up? I know it's difficult these days, but anything coming up that we might have a close look at?

> [*I like to help the person select a future example of their problem to work with to help them implement any solution we arrive at in the same situation.*]

Carolyn: Yeah. There will be a presentation that I will have to deliver a little bit further on in the year, perhaps June/July time.

Windy: Would you like to take that example so that we can work with that, so you can help yourself to prepare for that?

Carolyn: Yeah, that would be great.

Windy: So, tell me just a little bit about the presentation that you've got to give and the context in which you've got to give it?

Carolyn: It's a presentation about stress.

Windy: Just the way, isn't it?

Carolyn: Yeah, and me and my colleagues take it in turns in delivering this presentation. I'm new to this role in this job that I'm in and the presentation was delivered about three weeks ago and I went along and shadowed the person who was giving the presentation. So, I sat there and I watched them do it and they seemed really confident, they spoke really clearly and everybody was engaged in what they were saying. And I set myself a little challenge while I was in there: I'd said to this person prior to the presentation that, if I got the opportunity to say something, I would like to, because, if I came out of there having not said anything at all, I'd be really disappointed in myself. So, I said something that lasted about 20 seconds and, in that 20 seconds, my lips were quivering as if I was going to cry, my face went red, I was shaking and I was overwhelmed with all of the physical symptoms of anxiety that it feels me with dread if I was going to do it on my own.

Windy: Right, but you are going to do this on your own?

Carolyn: Yes, I would do, yeah.

Windy: OK. So, is this going to be an online presentation, do you think?

Carolyn: No, it's not. We're in a massive room where people are spaced from each other.

Windy: So, if I was to ask you, if I could give you one ingredient that wouldn't mean that you don't give the talk, but if I could give you one ingredient that would help you to eliminate your anxiety or at least reduce it to the point that you would be happy with, what would that ingredient be?

[I call this 'Windy's Magic Question' (WMQ). The opposite of the ingredient is frequently what the person is most disturbed about or their adversity.]

Carolyn: ... *[Pause]* I'm torn between it's really important to me to be able to speak clearly and make sense with what I'm delivering and, when I feel anxious, I feel like that doesn't happen.... So, something around that.

Windy: OK. So, if you knew, for example, that you were going to speak clearly and you would make sense to yourself and to the group, what difference would that make to you?

Carolyn: I imagine it would lessen the physical symptoms of the anxiety and make me feel perhaps a bit more confident or come across more confident with what I'm talking about.

Windy: Right, OK. So, we have to add a bit of confidence in there as well, don't we?

Carolyn: OK, yeah.

Windy: So, the ingredients are, let's be clear: confidence, clarity and what was the other one?

Carolyn: Well, clarity.

Windy: Making sense.

Carolyn: Yeah.

Windy: OK, confidence, clarity and making sense.

Carolyn: Yeah.

Windy: How often have you given talks before?

Carolyn: Not very often.

Windy: What, 20 times?

Carolyn: No, far less than that. In my previous job, I probably did it about… 10 times, but that was over 10 years ago.

Windy: OK. And how were you then giving talks?

Carolyn: Pretty much the same, really.

Windy: OK.

[*I wanted to see if Carolyn had any success experiences in giving talks with respect to her anxiety.*]

Carolyn: Yeah.

Windy: So, clarity, confidence and making sense – that's important to you.

Carolyn: Yeah.

Windy: And, so, I guess the threat would be not making sense, not being clear and not being confident.

Carolyn: Yeah.

[*The WMQ revealed that Carolyn was anxious about not making sense, not being clear and not being confident.*]

Windy: If that happened, and let's assume the worst temporarily because, if I can help you to deal with that, then would that help you going forward?

Carolyn: Yes.

Windy: OK. So, if you weren't clear, if you didn't make sense and you weren't confident, are you more concerned about how you would judge you or how other people would judge you? For example, let's say that I gave you another guarantee that, even though you came across as not being clear, confident or making sense, the audience wouldn't think badly of you, would that make a difference?

[*In public speaking the person may be more anxious about not living up to their standards or about being judged by others.*]

Carolyn: I think there's a bit of a mixture there with that.... [*Pause*] I guess if I had to choose between the two, it would be more important to me that I came across to others as being that way and that they received that... as opposed to... me being frustrated with it. I suppose it's more important for me to feel that they've heard and understood what I'm talking about.

[*It is clear then that the role of others is primary here.*]

Windy: OK. Because, if they don't understand what you've been talking about, if, in their view, you haven't been clear and you haven't come across very confidently, what would that mean to you?

Carolyn: ... [*Long pause*] I think it would make me feel... like I'm not good enough.

Windy: That would or you would?

Carolyn: … Yeah, I would.

[This interchange shows that Carolyn's attitude that she is not good enough is at the core of her anxiety and that she recognises that she makes herself 'feel' that way.]

Windy: You would. So, it's possible to actually have that experience of not being confident, not being clear and not making sense, and have a different emotion about that other than not being good enough. Is that right?

[Here I establish with Carolyn the possibility of holding a different attitude towards the same adversity.]

Carolyn: Yeah.

Windy: So, tell me a little bit about you: do you work as a counsellor?

Carolyn: Yeah, I do.

Windy: Can I ask you a personal question?

Carolyn: You can if you like.

Windy: Do you have children?

Carolyn: I do, yeah.

[*A useful intervention in single-session work is to determine whether or not the person would teach another group of people the attitude that underpins their problem (in Carolyn's case her clients or her children) and if not, what would they tech them. I could have explored the client route before asking about her children.*]

Windy: OK. So, imagine this scenario, if you will: a client comes in and says, 'I've got this issue that I'm anxious about – giving a public speech,' and you say, 'No, no, now, wait a minute. So, listen, you better make sure you come across to these people clearly, confidently and that they understand, because otherwise you won't be good enough as a person,' is that the kind of counselling you practise, by the way?

Carolyn: No.

Windy: You don't?

Carolyn: No.

Windy: If you were to encapsulate the message that you would want them to take away from the work about how to view themselves if they don't come across confidently, clearly and making sense, what would it be?

Carolyn: Can you put that across again?

Windy: Yes. Obviously I wasn't being clear. I was saying that, if you'd want them to take away something from the session with you about the meaning of not being clear, confident or making sense in terms of what that means for them as a person, what would you want them to take away from the counselling?

Carolyn: ... [*Pause*] Well, I certainly wouldn't want them to go away feeling like that means that they're not good enough.

Windy: OK. So, we know that you wouldn't want them to take that away.

Carolyn: Yeah.

Windy: What would you want them to take away, since we don't exist in a vacuum in terms of how we view ourselves?

Carolyn: ... I mean, ideally, in an ideal situation, to feel perhaps a bit empowered maybe that... [*pause*] they could do that, that they could... give that presentation and they could come across feeling clear and confident and making sense.

Windy: I can understand why you'd want, but, in order to do that, you have to help them to deal with the negative. You're wanting them to bypass that negative, aren't you?

[People often want to bypass dealing with an adversity as a way of solving their problem. My response is to help them to face and deal with the adversity.]

Carolyn: ... Yeah. I don't know, maybe having some understanding around the fear.

[It is clear that Carolyn does not know how to help people deal with adversity so, I invite her to hear my suggestion.]

Windy: OK. So, would you like to hear my therapeutic suggestion?

Carolyn: Yeah.

Windy: Encouraging them to accept themselves as an ordinary, fallible human being who can allow themselves to do well and not so well.

Carolyn: ... Yeah.

Windy: And maybe, once they've done that, they can use that as a foundation to be empowered to learn to be more confident, etc. Could you imagine that as a possible solution to your client's issue?

Carolyn: ... Yeah. It's something around having some kind of acceptance.

Windy: Yeah, acceptance of yourself as somebody who can both do well in a public setting and not. It sounds like what you're really saying is that it's extraordinarily important for you, right from the beginning, to be confident, clear and make sense.

Carolyn: Yeah.

Windy: And it sounds like a lot of pressure that you're putting on yourself there.

Carolyn: Yeah. Yeah.

Windy: So, what would it sound like if you took the pressure off but still regarded it as something not that great, but with a dose of self-acceptance thrown in for good measure? What would that sound like for you?

Carolyn: Well, it certainly would take the pressure off, maybe to not have such strong expectations of... [*pause*] myself, really, I suppose. I think it's... just recognising that I am... human and that it's OK, maybe? I don't know, it's OK?

              [*I often find that people want to feel 'OK' about an adversity when it is actually unpleasant.*]

Windy: Well, it's unpleasant.

Carolyn: Yeah.

Windy: If I can share something with you, I used to have a very bad stammer and I can remember occasions in school where I used to stand up and be anxious about the prospect of stammering, but later on in life I actually learnt to stop demanding that I be fluent and allowed myself to stammer, and that took a lot of the pressure off because I did allow myself. I didn't like stammering. It wasn't OK. It was unpleasant, but it allowed me to incorporate that into my own quite complex view of myself.

[Relevant self-disclosure can be a useful way to make a therapeutic point in single-session work.]

Carolyn: Yes. Yeah, that makes sense. So, would there be something around being perhaps a bit more open with myself about the way that I feel about it?

Windy: Yeah, actually open in two ways: one is open to yourself, because what you're trying to do is to shut that off – you're really saying, 'I want to eliminate the possibility that I can not be clear and they may not understand, I want to eliminate that,' of course you can't, so you're engaged in that. So, you could really be open with yourself and say, 'I'm going to strive to be as clear as I can. I don't always have to succeed.' And it's also possible, in a way, that you can actually be open with your audience.

Carolyn: Yes.

Windy: 'I present myself to you as a fallible human being who's nervous at the moment.'

Carolyn: Yeah. That's interesting.

Windy: Incidentally, that's a good way of taking the stress. In a way, you'll be teaching them personally how to de-stress yourself about a situation that you're anxious about.

[Anxiety thrives in an environment where the person seeks to eliminate experience or hide it from others. I also suggest that Carolyn can use her personal experience in her presentation on stress.]

Carolyn: Yep, and that's interesting because that 20 seconds when I did speak, it was in relation to a word cloud that was up on the screen where were loads of different words to do with anxiety, and one of the words in amongst that was fear. So, in the 20 seconds that I spoke, I said that I resonated with fear because I was fearful of speaking at the presentation, but that's as much as I could say before the physical symptoms took over and I thought, 'I can't say any more.'

Windy: What were the physical symptoms, Carolyn?

Carolyn: The strongest one for me is my lips wobble, you know like if you're just about to start crying?

Windy: Yeah.

Carolyn: And that's something that is really strong and I feel that everybody must be able to see it.

Windy: Yeah, OK. So, are you trying to stop yourself from doing that?

Carolyn: Possibly, yeah.

Windy: What would it be like if you allowed your lips to wobble, both actually and in your mind?

Carolyn: … [*Pause*] I think I'd just be embarrassed.

Windy: OK, because you'd be revealing what about yourself?

Carolyn: I'd be revealing the fact that I'm nervous and that it's on show.

Windy: And which means what about you?

Carolyn: … I don't know. What does it mean?

Windy: Well, it either means that you're not good enough or it means that you're a fallible human being who's struggling with an issue.

Carolyn: Right, OK, yeah. And I'd rather it be that I'm a fallible human being.

Windy: Right. In my book, if you really say, 'Oh my God, my lips are wobbling, I've got to stop them, I've got to stop them,' as opposed to, 'My lips are wobbling, I don't like it, but I'm going to allow them to wobble,' which of those two attitudes are going to lead you to think that everybody's going to notice your lips wobbling?

Carolyn: The first one.

Windy: That's how the mind works in anxiety, you see. Because you're so desperate to stop it, you think that other people are drawn to that particular lip. So, listen, why don't you summarise the work that we've done today?

[In this segment, I show Carolyn that she can apply the ideas we already discussed to her lips wobbling. I also show her that her fixed attitude towards this leads her to think that everybody will notice this while her more flexible attitude won't have this effect.]

Carolyn: You're asking me to summarise the session?

Windy: Yeah. It's a good counsellor strategy, to get the client to summarise.

Carolyn: Yeah. I'd summarise it by it's been really helpful for me to actually take part and be a volunteer. It's been really helpful for the understanding of that acceptance of being a fallible human being and that maybe it's OK to allow myself to let my lips wobble and perhaps realise that what I'm feeling is on view is perhaps not as strong as what people can see.

Windy: Right. But, even if they could see it, is that going to change your fallibility?

Carolyn: ... No.

Windy: Because people heard me stammer.

Carolyn: ... Yeah.

Windy: And I had to grapple with that and really use that as an opportunity to work towards greater self-acceptance.

[I add that Carolyn can work towards greater self-acceptance even if others see her lips wobble in the same way I did when others heard me stammer.]

Carolyn: Yeah. That's really interesting.

Windy: OK, shall we stop there and see what the group have got to say?

Carolyn: Yeah, thank you.

Windy: My pleasure.

Carolyn's Reflections (07-05-21)

I was quite nervous as the session began, I wanted to test myself and see how I might address an issue that I have pretty much carried all my working life around public speaking/giving presentations. Windy recognises the centre of my anxiety is around my self-belief of not feeling good enough and his first few questions allow us both to identify what I have difficulty with, what is the biggest area of concern and what I would like to take away from the session. This was very helpful. I wasn't expecting him to wave a magic wand and undo my core belief of not feeling good enough, however, I hoped that I would be able to find something that would be useful to think about before and during the dreaded presentation, to help with my anxiety. Windy made this clear which helped me to see my expectations of the single session were realistic. I found that when he reflected back to me what the threat was (to not make sense, not be clear and to not be confident) I knew we both had a clear understanding of what we were working with.

On reflection it seems that Windy was wondering whether to use my experience of being a mother or my experience of being a counsellor to identify what I might teach others in relation to my attitude with this issue, perhaps to notice something I may or may not be doing in my work with others in order to help myself (whether that be my children or my clients). I would have preferred to have gone with my experience of being a mother. I have 24 years' experience of motherhood and I am newly qualified as a counsellor. Therefore, being asked this question during a demonstration in front of many people (who I imagine would be in the field of counselling), I found quite difficult. Although I completely understood the rationale for this, I was mindful of being judged for my answer or how I would come across to the viewers of not being good enough. I felt the anxiety increase, I felt some pressure (from myself) to get this right and my concentration went out of focus. Which, interestingly, is the issue! I do work with clients who experience adversity and I help them to explore, face and find a way to manage whatever the issue might be. In the face of my adversity, which is delivering presentations, I still have my difficulties, perhaps that is my newfound self-acceptance!

It was helpful to be reminded of openness and acceptance, to recognise the unpleasantness of how I feel while presenting and in the lead up to. It is really interesting how the structure of SST and how Windy navigates the session left me with lots to reflect on afterwards. Some of it pleasant and some of it not so pleasant, I'm ok with that. The term 'I'm a fallible human being' may even become my new mantra!

12

Helping the Person to Trust that Her Mother Will Say One Thing and Do Another

Windy – Cathryn: Interview on 09/10/20
Time: 18 minutes 9 secs

Windy: What's your understanding about the purpose of our conversation?

Cathryn: I guess for me it would be to maybe gain a bit more understanding. I struggled to actually logon to start with so I missed the first 10–15 minutes of your presentation, but I got the end of it. So, I think I'm gathering what it's about around issues with parents.

Windy: And, so, you'd like to discuss an issue that you have with one or both of your parents?

Cathryn: One. I lost my dad nine years ago, so this is really about my relationship with my mum.

Windy: OK. And, so, if we were to have what for you is a successful conversation, what would you have achieved at the end of it?

[*Once again I ask for the person's session goal.*]

Cathryn: Probably a little bit of peace for myself as much as anything and just acceptance, I think.

Windy: So, you would like to experience peace and acceptance in relation to your mother.

Cathryn: Yeah.

Windy: OK. Well, can you help me to understand what for you is the difficulty with your mother?

Cathryn: Yeah. I think mainly it's around trust. It's a very long story so I'll try and cut it short. I'm the eldest of four siblings. I have one half-brother who is the youngest one. My mum actually left us when I was 15 and a lot went on in between but she actually came back and my parents were remarried eight years later and that's when she brought my half-brother with her. So, during that time, it wasn't a nice time, but we kind of got on with it.

    Then, in 2009 my dad developed cancer and he died in 2011. He had instructed me about a will that he had sorted out and expected, basically, my mum to stick to it. Long story short, she didn't. She changed it. So, there was quite a big argument around the family with the changes that she made, and she is very, very different with my youngest half-brother compared to the three of us who are my age.

[Here Cathryn alludes to 'trust' as a state that one experiences where a person is expected to stick to some kind of agreement and does so. I mention this here because a different form of 'trust' forms the centrepiece of the ensuing conversation.]

Windy: Can you help me to understand what the difference is?

Cathryn: Well, there's 21 years between me and my youngest brother. Obviously, he has a different father, but he is very, very different to the three of us. She overcompensates for him. I think she feels that the three of us leave him out to a degree. So, she will do anything to over-compensate for him and, because he is a very different personality, he makes sure he tells her when he's got issues with her around us, but the three of us don't really do that. She has lied to me in the past, I do know that. But, when my dad died, just before he died, me being the eldest he actually asked me if I would make sure my mum was OK and look after her, which I agreed to but I find quite difficult. She is getting a lot older now... so, I feel some responsibility, but I do struggle with being able to trust her and accepting some of the things that she's done.

Windy: So, you're struggling to trust her?

Cathryn: Hmm-mmm [yes].

Windy: How do you define trust in this sense?

Cathryn: ... Believe in her, I guess. Believe in what she says. I think she thinks she treats all of us the same in terms of, not particularly material stuff, but what she does for us, which isn't obviously as much now. Because she is getting older, she needs a lot more practical help than she used to. She's 75 now. And it's always the three of us, as I say, the three full siblings that she asks for, because my youngest sibling is really rubbish with practical-type stuff, so she never asks him. But she still will put herself out for him in terms of sticking up for him when she thinks there's an issue with the rest of us.

[*Note again that Cathryn alludes to a congruence between what a person says and what they do. If they that they will do 'x' then they will do 'x'.*]

Windy: Right. But your main issue is in terms of trust and lack of acceptance, would you say?

Cathryn: Mmm [yes].

Windy: So, just coming back to trust, it sounds like there's a mismatch between what she says and what she does.

Cathryn: Yes.

Windy: Is that?

Cathryn: I feel that's the case, yeah.

Windy: Yeah, OK. So, is that in a case in a number of areas or in particular areas?

Cathryn: Yeah, it is quite a lot of different areas and it can be very confusing.

Windy: Yeah. So, can I just share with you an idea that I often think about when it comes to this? I'd be interested to have your feedback on it. That actually you can trust that she will do something which is different than what she says. Do you understand what I mean by that?

[Here I share with Cathryn a very different form of 'trust'. Here you can 'trust' that a person will say one thing and do something different if that occurs in reality. Thus if a person says that they will do 'x' and they do 'y' then they can be expected to do what is different from what they say they will do. I introduce this idea to promote acceptance in Cathryn which is one of her stated session goals.]

Cathryn: Yeah.

Windy: That you can trust that there's going to be that kind of difference.

Cathryn: Yes.

Windy: Which is looking at trust in a somewhat different way, isn't it?

Cathryn: Yeah, I guess it is. I hadn't thought about it that way.

Windy: Yeah? Just reflect on that a minute and just tell me what you think of that as an idea.

           [*Counsellors often think there is little time in single-session work to encourage client reflection. This is not the case.*]

Cathryn: … [*Pause*] I guess I've always had a very strong view of my mum and what she does. So, I hadn't thought about it in those terms. So, maybe it's me thinking about in a slightly different perspective in that I have to accept that it could be different to what I believe it is.

Windy: Yeah, from her perspective it sounds like she says something, and we don't have access to her mental space, but, from your perspective, there is a difference between what she says and what she does. And, so, if you said, 'Actually, in certain areas I can trust that my mother will not do what she says she's going to do,' in a way.

Cathryn: Yeah.

Windy: Do you see what I'm saying?

Cathryn: Yeah, that's true.

Windy: Yeah.

Cathryn: Yeah, I can trust that that will probably happen more often than not.

[Cathryn indicates that she is beginning to use this different concept of 'trust' to re-think matters pertaining to her mother.]

Windy: Yeah.

Cathryn: Yeah.

Windy: So, I know that you would like to trust that there would be a match between what she says and what she does, but it sounds like the reality is that that is not the case. Would that help you to accept her more, if you reminded yourself, 'Well, I'm afraid I've got a mother who it sounds like she's going to say one thing and do another'?

Cathryn: I guess I have to.

Windy: Well, no, you don't. You could actually choose not to accept it. You could choose to disturb yourself about it and not accept it. You have a choice of disturbance or non-disturbance.
[This is an important point. I show Cathryn that she does not 'have to' accept reality. Rather, she has choices as outlined above.]

Cathryn: And obviously I'd rather have the non-disturbance.

Windy: You would? OK.

Cathryn: Yeah.

Windy: That's good. OK. So, what would help you? First of all, how would you disturb yourself about that discrepancy between what she does and what she says? If you were to disturb yourself about that, how would you do that?

Cathryn: I guess by not accepting by what she's saying and confronting her with, 'Actually, you said this and you've done this,' I think, because I'm the eldest sibling and I'm the one who tends to challenge her more than the others, especially since becoming a counsellor definitely; I see things very differently.

Windy: And what's the point of that challenge?

Cathryn: ... To let her know that I know she's not behaving appropriately, I guess, or that she's gone against what she said she would do.

Windy: OK. And how does she respond to that?

Cathryn: ... Now she lets me have a rant, if that's what I want to do, and challenge her. She will listen to me and maybe she doesn't always agree with me and certainly will not very often change her opinion or change what she's done, but I guess at least I can go away with, 'Well, she knows how I feel.'

Windy: OK. Now, I wonder if you can imagine doing that with acceptance rather than without acceptance; without disturbance rather than with disturbance. To have what I've called in the lecture a healthy unhappiness about your mother.

[*In the lecture that preceded this conversation entitled 'Dealing with Difficult Parents Using Single-Session Therapy', I discussed the concept of 'healthy unhappiness' where a person dislikes a state of affairs with respect to a parent, but does not disturb themself about it.*]

Cathryn: Yeah. When I saw that, that slide, I just thought that's kind of where I sit with her a lot of the time and I have done really since we lost my dad. That's exactly where I sit with her.

Sometimes I can get on with it and other times it's not very comfortable.

Windy: Right. So, I'm sort of outlining a process whereby she says something, she does something different, you acknowledge that: 'Oh, well, that's what I trust. I expect that from my mother. I don't like it. I'm going to call her on it. I'm going to request that she doesn't do that and she may or may not respond to my request for change.'

Cathryn: Rarely does she respond to my request for change.

Windy: Rarely, 'But at least I know that I've actually done what I can do.'

[*Often when a person has a difficulty with a parent a healthy it is important that they focus on what they can control – their own behaviour – rather that on what is out of their control – their parent's behaviour.*]

Cathryn: Yeah.

Windy: Right? Now, are you doing that at the moment? I mean, you say that there was a time where you felt comfortable about it. The way I see it, since you're not getting what you want, you're not going to be comfortable about it, are you?

Cathryn: No.

Windy: This is something that is an area of discomfort for you.

Cathryn: I guess I get a bit conflicted around it because I see how she behaves and that is so directly opposed to how I am with my own children, who are grown-ups now.

Windy: And why is that a conflict for you?

Cathryn: Because it doesn't sit right with me, how she behaves with us, particularly with me being the eldest, in comparison. It just doesn't sit right with me. It's like, if she cares or loves us like she says she does, how can she possibly behave that way.

Windy: Well, is it possible for her to care in her sense of caring?

[Here I introduce the possibility that Cathryn's mother may have a different sense of caring than Cathryn does.]

Cathryn: Possibly.

Windy: And still treat you the way that she treats you?

Cathryn: She says she does. She does say that she does love us all the same and that hasn't changed. Sometimes I find that quite hard to believe.

Windy: Right.

Cathryn: But, yes, I guess you're right. Yeah.

Windy: I mean, it might not be experienced by you as caring, and that's what I'm hearing, because you refer your own experience to your relationship with your kids. So, she doesn't match up to that, but, whether she cares or not, I don't know, but is it possible that she might, in her terms, care for you but in a way that you don't experience?

[Here I distinguish between Cathryn's mother's form of caring and Cathryn's own experience of being cared for which is influenced by a her own form of caring.]

Cathryn: Yeah, I think so.... Yeah, I think that's exactly what it is.

Windy: Yeah. And it's how you mind that discrepancy, how you negotiate that discrepancy.

Cathryn: Yeah, I guess I have to suspend that I am me and therefore I operate in one way and she's somebody very different.

Windy: Yeah, that's right. That, unfortunately, your mother doesn't have to be as caring towards you as you are as caring towards your kids.

Cathryn: ... Yeah, and possibly the way I am with my kids is a direct reflection of what I didn't get or what I missed.

Windy: You know, that's very interesting. I find that a lot. People often say, 'Well, if you experience this kind of parenting, then you're bound to repeat it,' but I often find that, in a way, what you're saying, that your parent has actually given you a role model of what not to do.

                [I mention this a lot in counselling and particularly in my single-session work.]

Cathryn: Yes.

Windy: And is that what you're saying?

Cathryn: Yeah, absolutely.

Windy: Yeah.

Cathryn: Yeah.

Windy: So, let me ask you a difficult question, if I may?

Cathryn: OK.

Windy: Can I ask you a difficult question?

Cathryn: Yeah.

[It is helpful to prepare a person before asking them a 'difficult' question.]

Windy: Why does your mother have to show you and your siblings the same care as you show to your children?

Cathryn: Why does she have to?

Windy: Why is it mandatory that she does that?

Cathryn: ... *[Pause]* I guess it isn't, is it?

Windy: You know something, if it was mandatory, she'd have to do it.

[This portion of the conversation is where I am most influenced by my work in Rational Emotive Behaviour Therapy by encouraging Cathryn to examine the demand that she holds towards her mother.]

Cathryn: Yeah.

Windy: She'd have to say, 'I don't really want to say this to my child, but some force of nature is making me say it to her.'

Cathryn: Yeah. I guess it isn't, is it? She's a totally different person to me, so she will see things from a very different perspective.

Windy: And that is sad because you're not getting the mothering and the parenting that you want. I get that.

[*Sadness is a form of 'healthy unhappiness' mentioned earlier.*]

Cathryn: Even at the age that I am, yeah.

Windy: It doesn't matter. It's interesting, I've talked about my Uncle Sid before – every time I talk to my Uncle Sid, he complains about being neglected by his brother, my father, when he was 12 or 13. Age doesn't matter.

[*My dear Uncle Sid died on 2 April 2021, aged 100. Eighty-seven years on he still felt hurt about his brother's past neglect*]

Cathryn: It's how you feel at the time.

Windy: Exactly. Right.

Cathryn: Yeah. Yeah.

Windy: So, do you want to summarise where we've got to so far here?

[*As we are approaching the end of the session, I ask the person to summarise the work we did in the session*]

Cathryn: I think, for me, what I've got out of it so far is that she doesn't have to be the same way as me and she isn't going to because she's a different person and maybe I need to accept that, even though she does one thing and says something different, that that is something, and around the trust issue, that I have to accept that that is how it is for me rather than making it more complicated and more difficult for myself.

[*This summary shows quite clearly that Cathryn has grasped the essence of the session. We often do our clients a disservice when we summarise for them.*]

Windy: Right. And still allow yourself to feel sad about it because you're not getting something which is important to you.

[*I do at times add an important point that the person has omitted from their summary.*]

Cathryn: Yeah. So, still recognising how it affects me as well.

Windy: Yeah.

Cathryn: Yeah.

Windy: How would that takeaway affect how you deal with your mother differently perhaps? How do you think you might influence your behaviour towards her?

[*Encouraging the person to think how they can implement the takeaway is often important in single-session work.*]

Cathryn: ... [*Pause*] Maybe be a bit more patient in terms of not expecting her to be like me and accepting that she is a very different person and that is maybe OK.

Windy: I would say expecting her to be like her.

Cathryn: Yeah. Yes. Yeah, I like that: expecting her to be like her.

Windy: Right, OK. So, have you got what you wanted from this session?

Cathryn: To be honest, at the beginning I didn't think I would because I've been so ingrained in how I felt about her for so long, but, actually, yeah, I can see slightly differently now. I think I've been so close to it, I haven't been able to see any further than I do.

[*This conversation lasted a little over 18 minutes. Cathryn's comment shows that it is possible to effect some change in long-standing 'ingrained' patterns in a short period of time.*]

Windy: Yeah. It's useful to talk to somebody and get an opportunity to stand back. But I think what also came across to me is that you do have the flexibility of mind in order to stand back and do that.

Cathryn: I do now. I didn't a few years ago, but I think I do more now. And, obviously, I would rather have some sort of a decent relationship with her than a really difficult one, especially as she's getting older, and we're not all perfect, are we? We're people who make mistakes.

Windy: Right, OK. Well, it'll be interesting to hear from you as a result of putting that insight into practice. Thank you very much for talking to me.

Cathryn: Thank you.

Cathryn's Reflections (18-05-21)

I have just re-read through the transcript and reflected on how I have moved forward since our session. There are times I still get angry and frustrated with my mum, but, on the whole, I do feel more accepting. I have gained awareness and understanding around my own expectations and behaviours. Although the 15-year-old me is still very angry with her, due to needs not being met at that time. I now feel more peaceful in terms of changing my rigid perspective of my mum.

I honestly didn't believe this session would influence my perception and responses as much as is evident to me now. Thank you. It was very inspiring working with you.

References

Frank, J. D. (1961). *Persuasion and Healing: A Comprehensive Study of Psychotherapy.* Baltimore, MD: The Johns Hopkins Press.

Hoyt, M. F., Bobele, M., Slive, A., Young, J., and Talmon, M. (eds) (2018). *Single-Session Therapy by Walk-In or Appointment: Administrative, Clinical, and Supervisory Aspects of One-at-a Time Services.* New York: Routledge.

Hoyt, M. F., and Talmon, M. F. (eds) (2014). *Capturing the Moment: Single Session Therapy and Walk-In Services.* Bethel, CT: Crown House Publishing.

Hoyt, M. F., Young, J., and Rycroft, P. (2020). Single session thinking 2020. *Australian & New Zealand Journal of Family Therapy, 41*(3), 218–30.

Hoyt, M. F., Young, J., and Rycroft, P. (eds) (2021). *Single-Session Thinking and Practice in Global, Cultural, and Familial Contexts: Expanding Applications.* New York: Routledge.

Keller, G., and Papasan, J. (2012). *The One Thing: The Surprisingly Simple Truth behind Extraordinary Results.* Austin, TX: Bard Press.

Simon, G. E., Imel, Z. E., Ludman, E. J., and Steinfeld, B. J. (2012). Is dropout after a first psychotherapy visit always a bad outcome? *Psychiatric Services, 63*(7), 705–7.

Slive, A., McElheran, N., and Lawson, A. (2008). How brief does it get? Walk-in single session therapy. *Journal of Systemic Therapies, 27*, 5–22.

Talmon, M. (1990). *Single Session Therapy: Maximising the Effect of the First (and Often Only) Therapeutic Encounter.* San Francisco: Jossey-Bass.

Young, J. (2018). SST: The misunderstood gift that keeps on giving. In M. F. Hoyt, M. Bobele, A. Slive, J. Young and M. Talmon (eds), *Single-Session Therapy by Walk-In or Appointment: Administrative, Clinical, and Supervisory Aspects of One-at-a-Time-Services* (pp. 40–58). New York: Routledge.

Index

acceptance 79, 96–8, 133, 205, 206,
      210, 215–22, 229–31
   cacophony of feelings towards
      mother 101–19
   of self, develop plan for 173–93
      Agnes's reflections 191–3
      session with Agnes 173–93
   of self 211, 213
   unhappy 120
action plan 19
   help client develop 34, 41
administrative support 16–17
adolescence 52
adult children, difficulties with 38
adversity 74, 102, 198, 202, 204–6,
      213
agency, therapy 16
agonizing 63, 64, 79
anecdotes 100
anger 110, 231
anxiety 33, 38, 146, 148–51, 153,
      154, 192, 194–213
   see also performance anxiety
apologising 102, 104
apology 104, 107
appointment-based SST 15
armour, emotional 186–8
Asperger's syndrome 95
asserting boundary with father 120–36
attention 122, 123, 126, 170, 187, 192
audience 84, 201, 207
   online vii, viii, 38, 42, 184
   virtual vii
autonomy, respect for 59
avoidance 149, 150

babying 125
bad feelings 66, 77
behaviour(s) 15, 23, 123, 124, 130,
      131, 135, 156, 179, 186, 223,
      230, 231
   changing 173, 174
Birmingham, developing plan to
      accept self in 173–91
blocks 13, 60, 61, 125, 141

Bobele, M. 15, 233
boundary
   helping assert with father 120–36
      Natalie's reflections 136
      session with Natalie 120–36
break-ups 78
Brixton Prison 138
bullying 54

cacophony of feelings 101–19
cancer 104, 164, 215
care 74, 76–8, 97, 122, 161, 164, 183,
      224, 225, 227
career 72
caring 65, 70, 224–6
case formulation 16, 18
CBT see cognitive behaviour therapy
certainty, demanding 151
chairwork 33
challenging but not overwhelming 185
'chapters in book' metaphor 55
children 67, 68, 91, 92, 101, 121,
      132, 133, 202, 203, 212, 224, 227
   adult 38
Christianity 174
clarity 29–30, 173, 199, 200
client assessment 16
client-centred 24
client's strengths, identify and utilise
      30–1
cognition 15, 23
cognitive behaviour therapy (CBT)
      13, 99, 154, 190
comfort zone 88
commentaries on session work viii
commitment 140, 156
communication 29, 45, 46, 56, 60, 82,
      98, 136
concern 14–16, 19, 20, 24, 26, 27, 31,
      33, 38–41, 104, 212
   work to understand underlying
      process behind 40–1
compassion 31, 164, 167
compromised, being 67
confidence 190, 198–206, 212

congruence 105, 106, 166–8, 171, 217
connection, prompting mum for 80–100
    Carla's reflections 99–100
    session with Carla 80–100
continuous professional development
    (CPD) vii, viii, 11, 31, 37
conventional clinical thinking 20, 23, 34
conversations at Onlinevents 42, 43–231
    clarify purpose of 39
    framework for 39
    goal 40
    volunteers (named changed)
        Agnes 173–93
        Alison 101–19
        Carla 80–100
        Carolyn 194–213
        Cathryn 214–31
        Emma 157–72
        Grace 62–79
        Natalie 120–36
        Oscar 137–56
        Steph 45–61
    reflections by volunteers 42
        Agnes's 191–3
        Carla 99–100
        Carolyn 212–13
        Cathryn 231
        Emma 172
        Grace 78–9
        Natalie 136
        Oscar 156
        Steph 59–61
    set goal for 40
    transcripts of 42
    WD's comments on 42
core beliefs 212
counselling vii, 60, 73, 79, 106, 157,
    191, 192, 203, 204, 213, 226
    online 37
counsellors 15, 31, 37, 65, 66, 72, 73,
    157, 219
    training and education of vii, 72
courage 86–9, 91, 148
Covid-19 pandemic vii, 37, 93, 138, 143
CPD *see* continuous professional
    development
cults 174, 175, 177
culture 72

data collection 16
deadlines 138, 140–4, 154, 156

'Dealing with Difficult Parents Using
    Single-Session Therapy' 222
death 49, 52, 60, 81, 88, 103, 104,
    106, 149, 157, 215, 216, 228
decision 21, 62–4, 66, 75
    helping client make 26
demoralized, feeling 35
'difficult' questions 227
disappointment 177–82, 197
    to her mother 177
discomfort 47, 48, 50, 54, 56, 58, 224
disconnected, feeling 81, 92, 93
discrepancies 221, 225
doubts, reservations and objections
    (DROs) 17, 129
disloyal, being 51, 53
distraction 139, 184
distress 60, 101, 190
disturbance 100, 102, 122, 123, 198,
    221, 222
divorce 121
dread 110, 183, 197
DROs *see* doubts, reservations and
    objections
Dryden, Windy (WD) 45–231

early development 174
Ellis, Albert 95, 96, 100
embedded approach to SST 21–2
emotional impact 30
emotionality 81, 184
emotion(s) 15, 23, 30, 60, 68, 74,
    111, 136, 172, 202
empathy 31, 108, 164, 165, 167, 168
empowerment 56–8, 61, 204, 205
end of session goal 25
end session well 35–6, 42
    clarify next steps 35–6
    tie-up loose ends 35
engage client quickly through work 24
environmental resources 31
equality 59
evaluation 16
exclusion criteria 20
existentialism 137, 139, 155
expectations 146, 169, 206, 212, 231
    managing 60
    realistic 15
exposure, gradual 192
external resources 32, 41
Facebook 63, 64
failure 148, 150, 154, 159, 160

fallibility 205, 208–11, 213
family 91, 118, 121, 215
fear 53, 60, 61, 63, 65, 72, 78, 92, 93, 106, 110, 128, 156, 159, 161, 188, 196, 205, 208
feedback 36, 218
feelings 26, 27, 35, 56, 60, 66, 69, 77–82, 84, 86, 87, 89, 91, 124, 126, 136, 151, 166, 170, 171, 173, 175–8, 183, 190–2, 196, 204, 211, 212
    towards mother 101–19
flexible attitude 48, 73, 210
focus(ing)15, 16, 21, 22, 24, 26, 28, 30, 35, 40, 56, 59, 60, 71, 81, 89, 97, 108, 111, 112, 131, 136, 139, 150, 151, 166, 182, 213, 223
    agree for session with client 27, 40
    follow-up session 22, 36
forgiveness 103, 104, 108–13, 118
Frank, Jerome 35, 233
freedom 79, 144
friends 49, 51, 53–7, 63, 66, 69, 70, 74, 77–9, 95
frustration 103, 110, 121, 141, 142, 201, 231

gateway approach to SST 21–2
'giving in' 122
goals
    end of session 25–6
    outcome 19, 47, 173
    problem-related 26, 32, 33
    process 19, 47, 173
    session goal vs problem-related goal 26
    therapist's in SST 19
grief/grieving 60, 61, 161
guided imagery 58
guilt 38,
    helping person to address 62–80, 124, 176
    session with Grace 62–79
    Grace's reflections 78–9
happiness 99, 103, 104
harmony 111
hatred 110, 116, 118
healthy negative emotion 74
healthy unhappiness 222, 228

help(ing)
    determine best helping stance with client 25–6
    person to accept cacophony of feelings 101–19
    person to address performance anxiety 194–213
    person to address procrastination 137–56
    person to assert boundary with father 120–36
    person to get unstuck 45–61
    person to integrate different parts of herself 157–72
    person to trust mother will say one thing and do another 214–32
    provided quickly in response to help being sought 14
help-seeking 15, 35
hindsight 60
history-taking 16
honesty 75, 76, 79, 104, 105, 107, 230
Hoyt, M. F. 13, 15, 233, 234
humanistic counselling 60
humour 72, 82, 162, 166
hurt 82, 84, 87, 124, 228

illness 49, 52
imagery 33, 34, 58, 188
Imel, Z. E. 24, 233
inclusion criteria 20
indoctrination 174
informed consent, importance of 16
'ingredient' question 50, 51, 60, 198, 199
    see also Windy's Magic Question
inner world 84, 85, 87
insight vii, 156, 173, 231
integrating different parts of self, helping person
    Emma's reflections 172
    session with Emma 157–72
integrative psychotherapy 137
intellectual processing 184, 185
internal resources 41
interrupting 27, 40, 123, 125, 127
interviews *see* conversations at Onlinevents
intrapersonal solution 107, 108
irritation 128

judgment 53, 54, 61, 79, 176, 179

'Keep a-Knockin' But You Can't
    Come In' 135
keep on track 27–8
Keller, G. 26, 233
kick-started to do something, being
    158–9
kindness 31

Lawson, A. 21, 233
learning 29, 33, 36, 37, 72, 73, 79,
    106, 114, 116, 126, 131, 134,
    141, 145, 186, 205, 207
lectures vii, 72, 94, 222
lighter feeling 115, 116
'little girl', being treated like 121
lips wobbling 210
listening 17, 61, 79, 114, 121, 122,
    124, 126, 130, 131, 135, 136,
    169, 222
live therapy demonstrations (LTDs)
    vii, 11
lockdown 37, 94, 102, 176
loneliness 123
loose ends, tie up 35
loss 66, 74, 77, 78, 157
love 84, 105, 118, 128, 224, 225
loving 164
Ludman, E. J. 24, 233
lying 216

marriage 52, 121, 176
McElheran, N. 21, 233
mental health vii, 21
metacommunication 98
middle pathway 162
mistakes 178, 231
mode *see* number of sessions 13–14
morale, restore client's 35
mother 128, 134, 175, 177, 179–82,
    191, 212
    helping person accept cacophony
        of feelings towards 101–19
    relationship with 80–100
    trust she will say one thing and do
        another 214–31
motherhood 213
mothering 228
move forward, help client 35
moving house 64
mutual support 48

negative feelings 104
negotiating 74, 133, 225
    boundaries 133
    solution 32
nervousness 208, 209, 212
nominated concern/problem 14–16,
    24, 26, 31, 41
non-acceptance 181
non-disturbance 221
non-judgmental, being 79
not listening 124
number of sessions ('mode') 13
nurture of self 160, 168

obstacles 34, 37
    problem-solving of 41
OCD (obsessive compulsive disorder)
    88, 89
one-off single session 38
'one thing', principle of 25–6
one-way support 47
online events vii
Onlinevents
    conversations 42
    single-session therapeutic
conversation 38
    SST at Onlinevents 37–42
    what is Onlinevents? 37
    see also process view of SST
conversations at onlinevents
online presentations, SST 42
openness 213
ordinary person 70–2
organisational support 15–17
other-directed nature 166
other-rejection 180
outcome goals, therapist's 19, 47, 173
outdated view 90, 91
overcompensation 216

pain 60, 82, 85, 88, 189
painful feelings 60, 78, 83, 182
panic attacks 188
Papasan, J. 26, 233
parenting 226, 228
parents 38, 114, 120, 121, 128, 214,
    215, 222
performance anxiety
    helping person to address 194–213
    Carolyn's reflections 212–13
    session with Carolyn 194–213

perseverance 31
person centred counsellor 99
person centred therapy 13
personal experience 208
poor behaviour 130–1
power of 'now' 23–4
PowerPoint presentation viii, 38
pragmatic expectation 147
presentation, anxiety about delivering
    to groups 194
pre-session questionnaire 15
pressure 90, 140–4, 146, 152–4, 170,
    189, 206, 207, 213
prison 63, 138
privacy, need for 123
proactive, being more 159
problem(s) vii, viii, 14, 24, 26, 29,
    31–3, 40, 41, 67, 76, 102, 108,
    109, 122, 136, 145, 150, 156,
    164, 195, 196, 203, 205
    identify client's previous attempts
      to deal with 31–2
problem-related goal 26, 32, 33
process goals 19, 47, 173
process view of SST conversations at
    onlinevents 39–42
    agree focus, set goal for
      conversation, retain focus 40
    clarify purpose of conversation
      with client 39
    develop action plan and problem-
      solve obstacles 41
    end well 42
    identify solution and invite person
      to rehearse it in session 41
    and WD's therapeutic goals 39–42
    work to understand underlying
      process behind concern 40–1
procrastination 38,
    helping person to address 137–56
    Oscar's reflections 156
    session with Oscar 137–56
protection 128, 189
protective bubble 89
psychotherapy vii, 137
public speaking 192, 201, 212
purpose in life, re-finding 158
pushing someone away 93

Q&A period 28, 38
questionnaire, pre-session 15
questions 25, 38, 42, 60, 179, 212

Rational Emotive Behaviour Therapy 227
realistic expectations about SST 15, 23
recognition 69
re-education 135
referral to SST based on suitability
    assessment 20
reflect-digest-act-wait-decide process 36
reflections by volunteers on SST
    conversations 42
    Agnes's 191–3
    Carla 99–100
    Carolyn 212–13
    Cathryn 231
    Emma 172
    Grace 78–9
    Natalie 136
    Oscar 156
    Steph 59–61
regret 52, 61
rehearse solution, encourage client to 33
rejection 61, 92, 180
relationships 49, 52, 56, 59, 80, 84,
    85, 91, 94, 101, 120, 159,
    174–6, 190, 214, 225, 231
    therapeutic 24, 59
religion 174, 190, 192
rescuer mode 60
research 13, 16, 24
resilience 31
responsibility 20, 27, 46, 71, 76–8,
    89, 135, 152, 216
rigid attitudes 70, 74, 232
risk assessment 16
rituals 88
role-play 33
rules 135, 159
Rycroft, P. 13, 233

sadness 61, 108, 228, 229
schizophrenia 175
secrets 60, 61
self-acceptance 180, 182, 183, 188,
    206, 211
self-actualisation 182
self-compassion 167
self-disclosure 207
self-doubt 148, 151, 153
self-harming 164
self-help 31
self-judgment 179
sense, making 33, 47, 188, 189, 198–
    204, 206, 207, 212

service delivery 13, 20, 21, 26
session(s)
    goal vs problem-related goal 26
    number of ('mode') 33–4
sex offenders 63
sexual relations 45, 175
shame 38, 61, 173–8, 180, 183, 186, 190–2
sharing how you feel 85
shift
    in attitude 57, 115, 170, 178, 180, 181
    in conversation 184
    in focus 131
siblings 102, 215, 217, 221, 227
Simon, G. E. 24, 233
Single Session Therapy (Talmon, 1990) 11
single-session (aka 'one-off')
    therapeutic conversation 38
single-session therapy (SST) 11–36
    appointment-based 15, 39
    definition 12–13
    favourable conditions for 14–17
        both therapist and client hold realistic expectations about SST 15
        help provided at point of need 18
        help provided quickly in response to help being sought 14
        importance of informed consent 16
        organisational and administrative support is provided 15–17
        therapy begins immediately 16
        time between help-seeking and appointment used well 15
    fully contracted form of therapy 12
    nature of 13
    online presentations 42
    seeks to integrate two seemingly different positions 12–13
    therapeutic purpose 12
    therapist's goals 19
        therapist's outcome goals 19
        therapist's process goals 19
    three major foundations 13–14
    waiting list as oxymoron 14
    ways of delivering 20–2
        'gateway' or 'embedded' approach 21–2

single-session therapy (SST) (contd)
    integrate SST into agency's service provision 20
    walk-in SST 21
    see also Onlinevents
single-session mindset 23
single-session thinking
    agree focus for session with client 27
    arrange follow-up 36
    be clear and foster clarity 29–30
    be client-centred 24
    create realistic expectation for SST 23
    determine best helping stance with client 26–7
    develop end of session goal 25–6
        one thing 25–6
        session goal vs problem-related goal 26
    encourage client to rehearse solution 33
    encourage client to summarise 34–5
    encourage client to use environmental resources 31
    end well 35
        clarify next steps 35–6
        tie-up loose ends 35
    engage client quickly through work 24–5
    and good practice 23–36
    help client to develop action plan 34
    identify and utilise client's previous attempts to deal with problem 31–2
    identify and utilise client's strengths 30–1
    keep on track 27–8
    keep up good therapeutic pace and stop when finished 28
    make an emotional impact 30
    negotiate solution 32
    utilise power of 'now' 23–4
sleep problems 102–4,160, 161
Slive, A. 15, 21, 233, 234
social media 64
solution(s) 15, 19, 26, 27, 29, 31–4, 58–60, 62, 75, 108, 153, 196, 205
    encourage client to rehearse 33
    identify and invite person to rehearse it in session 41
    negotiate 32
    tweaking 33

sooner is better 18
sorry, saying 102
sparing person's feelings 82
spitefulness 102
spontaneity 94, 96, 98, 100
SST *see* single-session therapy
stammering 207, 211
Steinfeld, B. J. 24, 233
storytelling 136
strengths, client's 30–1
stressing 165
success 34, 37, 80, 126, 129, 130,
    132, 154, 200, 214
suffering 143, 148, 155
suicide 164
suitability assessment, referral to SST
    based on 20
summarise, encourage client to 34–5, 56
superwoman 78, 167, 168
    and little mouse in corner 162
support 16, 17, 31, 46–50, 52–4, 56,
    57, 60, 51, 66, 68–74, 77, 79,
    156, 189
supportive, being 70, 72, 73, 166
suppressed feelings, encouraging
    client to express 26
sympathy 164

Talmon, Moshe 11, 13, 15, 233, 234
teaching 114, 115, 125, 126, 132,
    133, 134, 203, 208, 212
Teams 87
tender-minded 31
theme, identify 40
therapeutic focus 30
therapeutic help 22
therapeutic pace 28
therapeutic purpose of SST 12
therapeutic relationship 24, 59
therapeutic stance 27
therapists 12–17, 21, 23–38, 174, 177
    goals in SST 19
    training and education of vii
therapy agency 16
throwing up (vomiting) 106
tough-minded 31
trainee counsellors 59, 192
training and education vii
trampled, feeling of being 186–8
transcript of conversation, permission
    to publish 42
transparency 39, 60

trust 20, 59
    mother will say one thing, do another
    Cathryn's reflections 231
    session with Cathryn 214–31
tweaking of solution 33
two-way support 47

unblocking 139
unconditional self-acceptance 182
understanding 12, 16, 17, 26, 27, 32,
    39, 41, 47, 61, 62, 68, 84, 93,
    98, 120, 173–5, 194, 205, 211,
    212, 214, 231
unhappy acceptance 120
unhealthy negative emotion 74
unstuck, help client get 11, 35
    session with Steph 45–61
    Steph's reflections 59–61
upsetting people 82, 83, 106

victims 60, 63
virtual audience 7
volunteering 62, 80, 173, 192, 195,
volunteers vii, viii, 28, 31, 38–40, 42
    conversations *see* conversations at
        Onlinevents
    names changed 42
    permission to publish transcript 42
    see also reflections by volunteers
        on SST conversations

waiting times to access relevant help 36
walk-in SST 15, 20, 21
walk-in therapy clinic 21, 39
wave of connection 85
WD *see* Dryden, Windy
Wilson, John viii
Windy's Magic Question (WMQ) 198
WMQ *see* Windy's Magic Question
workshops 11, 37, 59, 138
worry 82, 95, 105, 106

Young, J. 13, 15, 233, 234

Zoom vii, 121, 123, 126

Lightning Source UK Ltd.
Milton Keynes UK
UKHW021122150721
387213UK00008B/1636

Lightning Source UK Ltd.
Milton Keynes UK
UKHW021122150721
387213UK00008B/1636